SAN FRANCISCO

SAN FRANCISCO

A PROFILE WITH PICTURES

Barnaby Conrad

Bramhall House · NEW YORK

This edition published by Bramhall House,
a division of Clarkson N. Potter, Inc.,
by arrangement with The Viking Press, Inc.
(C)

Library of Congress catalog card number: 59-12453

Printed in the U.S.A.

CONTENTS

ACKNOWLEDGMENTS

The author would like to acknowledge the enthusiastic help of James DeT. Abajian, Librarian of the California Historical Society; the Pioneer Society of California; the Wells Fargo History Room; Frances Moffat of the San Francisco *Examiner*, Mildred Brown Robbins of the San Francisco *Chronicle*; Bill Young of the *Chronicle*; and the photo libraries of both newspapers.

Also I should like to point out that most of the photographs in this book were taken by members of the talented organization known as the Bay Area Photographers Society. To them and to the other photographers whose work is included, my heartfelt thanks.

—B.C.

To Dale

8

PROLOGUE

"San Francisco is a mad city inhabited by perfectly insane people whose women are of a remarkable beauty."

This was said by Rudyard Kipling half a century ago as he became Just Another Writer trying to answer the impossible question:

What is San Francisco and what is a San Franciscan?

Writers have been trying to answer this since the year San Francisco was born (which also happens to be the year the United States was born). Everyone's had a whack at it from President Taft ("The city that knows how") to Bret Harte ("Serene, indifferent of Fate") to an otherwise excellent fellow, New York columnist Leonard Lyons ("Nothing but a three-day city—including all the museums").

Another New Yorker, Mrs. Henry Simon, wife of the publisher, remarked to me recently that San Francisco "looked as though it had been constructed of blocks by a highly talented child."

And a Broadway producer breathed in theaterese as he gazed in awe at the view from the Top of the Mark, "Hate to go to sleep in this town—afraid they'll have struck the set by morning!"

Prizefighter Willie Britt summed up a great many people's feelings about our city when he shouted out fifty years ago, "I'd rather be a busted lamppost on Battery Street, San Francisco, than the Waldorf-Astoria!"

The quotes are endless.

My own idea of San Francisco is that it is a cosmopolitan labyrinth of infinite surprises. But *that* doesn't help much!

How to re-create San Francisco's special charm?

Can it be done in mere prose? Surely if O'Brien, Altrocchi, Caen, Jackson, Beebe, Lewis, and Gilliam can't do it in their excellent and varied books, no one can. To capture the physical sorcery of San Francisco I think one almost *has* to have recourse to photographs, which is what we've done in this book.

9

But then what about the sounds and the smells?

The ideal way to conjure up San Francisco would be to leaf through these pictures lazily with one tape recording playing columnist Herb Caen reading one of his marvelous "fog-seeping-through-the-Gate" essays, another tape giving out with cheery cable-car ding-da-da-ding dings, doleful foghorn moans, and assorted seal barkings, while a small boy operated an atomizer containing essence of summer fog, fresh crab, and a dash of roasting coffee.

Lacking these accessories, leaf through the book anyway and see if you can find your San Francisco in some of the photos. San Francisco is a personal thing, and each of us holds a different image of her inside. This is San Francisco to me, and it may not be San Francisco to you. For all I know, you may call it Frisco and prefer Los Angeles!

But I think that's unlikely somehow, for, if you did, why would you have picked up this book in the first place? One of the great unifying factors amongst San Franciscans, besides their deep love and fierce pride in their city, is their friendly disdain for everything Angelean—*Los* Angelean, that is. They feel, along with Herb Caen, "Isn't it nice that the kind of people who prefer Los Angeles to San Francisco live there?"

We revel, but not bitterly, in such anti-"L.A." comments as Orson Welles': "Drive as far as you like in any direction; wherever you find yourself it looks exactly like the road to an airport, *any* road to *any* airport."

Or that of Wilson Mizner, who once worked as a "professor" in a Barbary Coast brothel: "Los Angeles is a parking lot for used cities."

Or Lucius Beebe's: "Every time I find myself in Los Angeles I wonder what I've done to displease God."

Yes, we like our city better than Los Angeles, better than Chicago, better than New York. A San Franciscan isn't quite as smug as the Parisians who declare, "Why should I travel? I'm here!"—but he borders on it. He appreciates Gene Fowler's tribute, "Every man should be allowed to love two cities—his own and San Francisco."

Just what does one think of when one hears those two words San Francisco?

Hills? Cable cars? The bridges? The Golden Gate? Fog?

All those obvious things in a jumble, perhaps. But first—like most natives of this benign city—when I think of San Francisco I think of . . .

THE PAST

The Golden Gate. (Photo: E. Safran.)

Someone once said, "Every San Franciscan has one foot on a hill and the other in the past."

It's true. I can't believe that Seattle and Chicago and New York, for instance, wallow in their histories the way we San Franciscans do. And San Francisco, as a real city, is a young upstart compared to Boston, Philadelphia, New York, and New Orleans. Even Chicago had been incorporated for fifteen years by 1847, which is when San Francisco came around to naming itself officially.

11

Of course, its history is far older than that. The honor of being the first to see the site belonged to a Spanish expedition headed by Gaspar de Portolá (pronounced porto-*lah*); and this was in 1769. What a sight it must have been to them as they came up from the south over the Montara hills and suddenly became the first white men ever to gaze on the marvelous vista!

Spanish and English galleons had sailed past the Golden Gate in the sixteenth and seventeenth centuries; indeed, in 1579, Sir Francis Drake nailed a "Plate of Brasse to a Firme Post" nearby up the coast to declare that the area was part of "The Kingdome of Herr Majesty Queen Elizabeth of England and Herr Successors Forever." But none had discovered the harbor, perhaps because of heavy fogs shrouding the entrance. Finally, in 1775, just two months after the Battle of Bunker Hill, the bay was entered by the small Spanish packet *San Carlos*. Her captain, Don Manuel de Ayala, spent a month surveying the bay and then departed to tell of its beauty.

A year later Captain Juan Bautista de Anza arrived with less than two hundred settlers. He built the first building, an adobe house, which still stands in the present-day Presidio and is used as an officers' club. One month later the beautiful Mission Dolores was dedicated, called then San Francisco de Asís.

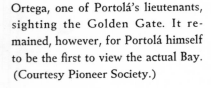
Ortega, one of Portolá's lieutenants, sighting the Golden Gate. It remained, however, for Portolá himself to be the first to view the actual Bay. (Courtesy Pioneer Society.)

For the first sixteen years the Spaniards did little toward building a city. They called it Yerba Buena because of the green mint that grew abundantly there, and were content to raise sheep and cattle. The proud Spanish families, many of whose descendants are active in the city today, lived on haciendas around the bay area and life was healthy and gay.

The end of the idyllic Spanish way of life came in 1846, when the Yankee ship *Portsmouth* sailed into Yerba Buena Cove and Commander John Montgomery of the United States Navy strode ashore to hoist the stars and stripes in the plaza now bordered by Kearny, Washington, and Clay Streets.

12

Although the Mexican general, Vallejo, did not put up a fight the Spanish did not submit to the new rule without pride and unpleasantness. A letter written by Montgomery to the American vice-consul the day before the American occupation is particularly interesting because of its Freudian slip: "I will be gratified to see him [the Mexican alcalde]

Yerba Buena, spring, 1837. The earliest known painting of San Francisco, or Yerba Buena, done by surveyor Jean Jacques Vioget. (Courtesy Wells Fargo Bank.)

pleasant on the occasion [of the occupation]." The commander, of course, intended to say "present"—or did he?

Julia Altrocchi writes of the humiliation to the Spanish settlers in her book, *The Spectacular San Franciscans* (New York: Dutton, 1949):

Gradually, by hook or crook (but chiefly by crook), the invaders made debtors and mortgagees of the Spanish ranch owners, and piece by piece took over the great golden valleys. In many instances the invaders simply squatted and refused to move.

The granddaughter of Rafaela Martinez and Dr. Tennent, Mrs. Mary Tennent Carleton, tells a significant little story of the final days of a daughter of the Domingo Peralta family. Don Domingo himself had been put to untold humiliations by squatters, threatened by cannon set up on his property, sued for trespass on his own land, thrown into jail because he had dared to cut down one of his own trees. His daughter's house, successor to the old adobe, was a beautiful two-story frame house, with balcony above, veranda below, in the Mediterranean style, and over all the trailing honeysuckles and the Jericho roses, almost as much beloved by the Spanish as the small, fragrant, pink Castilian roses. This had been an unusually happy ranch home for many years. But now that the widow and her sons and daughters had been left unprotected, the property had gradually drifted out of their hands into the clever clutch of the Yankee. The new possessors were due to come riding in at any minute. The horses of the Peralta family were waiting outside, several of them packed with the last belongings. As the mother of the family stood on the veranda, looking for the last time into the old home, she chanced to drop a remark about how much she had cherished the hardwood living-room floors which she and her mother before her had polished daily to a queen's-coach brightness. One of her sons,

13

Officers' club, the Presidio, the oldest building in San Francisco (1776). (Photo: Conrad.)

already astride his horse, hearing his mother's remark, immediately drove his mount up the steps and into the living room, and back and forth, with gouge-hooved frenzied patterns over the polished wood, turning it into a ridged barnlike floor.

"The Yankees shall not have our *home!* But they *may* have our *stable!"* he cried—an incident fraught with all the passion of the proud Spanish race, under the inescapable boot heels of the trampling pioneers.

In 1847 there were 450 people in the town, now officially named by the Town Council San Francisco. The way it came to be named is told by B. E. Lloyd, writing in 1876 in his *Lights and Shades:*

It is very possible that there are a few, if not many persons who are ignorant of the fact that San Francisco *town* did not exist until 1847. Previous to that year the few straggling huts that stood upon the site now occupied by San Francisco were called by the Spanish and Indian residents on the peninsula *Yerba Buena.* The origin of this name (which is the Spanish for *Good Herb*) was from a small, protected cove in the bay, upon which grew luxuriantly an herb of medicinal value, and therefore called *good* herb. The island now bearing the poetical title of "Goat" situated in the bay about midway between San Francisco and Oakland, and which every incoming train on the Central Pacific Railroad attempts to reach by thundering down "Long Wharf" at a fearful speed, apparently intent on leaping the intervening space and claiming the island by "squatter's" right—this Goat Island that was the subject of dispute between the "people" and the railroad, and inspired to eloquence or cutting sarcasm many indignation-meeting orators was also called Yerba Buena for the same reason, as was the little cove. And this is how, and why, the name was changed from Yerba Buena to San Francisco.

On the 30th of January, 1847, W. A. Bartlett (first alcalde of Yerba Buena) made proclamation as follows, through the columns of the *California Star:*

AN ORDINANCE

Whereas, the local name of Yerba Buena, as applied to the settlement or town of San Francisco, is unknown beyond the district; and has been applied from the local name of the

14

A typical California caballero riding over his land near San Francisco. The painting is by James Walker. (Courtesy Mrs. Reginald Walker.)

cove on which the town is built; Therefore to prevent confusion and mistakes in public documents, and that the town may have the advantage of the name given on the public map,

It is hereby ordained, that the name *San Francisco* shall hereafter be used in all official communications and public documents, or records appertaining to the town.

Wash'n A. Bartlett,
Chief Magistrate.

In 1848 the population had doubled, but after James Marshall stumbled on gold at Sutter's Mill in the Sierra Foothills only a few people remained in San Francisco; all those with the normal complement of legs and arms had headed for the gold country. By the end of the year 1849 the population had mushroomed to 25,000. People were flooding in from the East and the cove was a forest of masts of deserted ships whose crews had left to dig gold.

Prices soared. It's said that eggs were a dollar each. Sam Brannan, our city's first millionaire, made a good part of it selling shovels and supplies to the miners and arranging to send their laundry to Hawaii (then called the Sandwich Islands), where the cost was less than in San Francisco. Women were scarce, and the all-night types were paid as

15

A rare and historically exciting photo of Marshall standing near the spot at Sutter's Mill where he discovered the gold that started the stampede. (Photo: Pioneer Society.)

More than five hundred ships abandoned in 1851 by gold-seeking crews and passengers. This shot was taken by William Shew, from Rincon Point near the present corner of Spear and Harrison Streets.

much as $500 to $600 for their wares. When a boat arrived in the harbor the semaphore on Telegraph Hill would tell how many women were aboard, along with other cargo information. Crime was rampant; 4200 murders were committed in the mid-1850s. In 1851 there were only twelve constables and the alcalde to protect the population of 40,000. Finally, a committee of citizens, under the leadership of Brannan, took the law into their own hands, calling themselves the Vigilantes. Before disbanding five years later they lynched several murderers, deported scores of others, and convinced hundreds of petty crooks that they weren't wanted, and crime was suddenly no longer a major problem.

But the citizens were far from tamed. The day that California was made a state, September 9, 1850, touched off a fantastic celebration in San Francisco. One of the celebrants, Jim Savage, a young Princeton graduate who came across the plains in a covered wagon and became head of over five tribes of Indians, marched down the streets of San Francisco with twelve Indians and three squaws carrying a barrel of gold dust which they scattered on the streets.

By 1851 San Francisco had suffered six fires. Each time the town was razed and each time it was rebuilt. As a result the famous volunteer fire companies were started. There was violent competition between the Howard 3, the Knickerbocker 5, the Manhattan 2, and the Tiger 14 to see who could get to the fire first and put it out. Fires almost became social affairs; champagne was served to the volunteers on the Howard 3, and the Firemen's Balls were the most distinguished gatherings of the year. Volunteer name lists included such notables as Claus Spreckels, James Flood, and Lillie Hitchcock Coit (honorary member).

Wealthy Lillie was quite a gal, the darling of the firemen, the despair of her dozens of beaux who couldn't keep up with her, on or off one of her many horses, and always the object of the clucking tongues of saner folk. Notice that in the photograph below she is nonchalantly holding a bottle of booze, which nice girls just didn't *do* in those days.

Come to think of it, has it ever been *de rigueur*, before or since, to pose for one's formal portrait clutching one's hobby? Madcap Lillie was to leave her money for the creation of two monuments to her pals, the volunteer firemen of the city, and one of them, Coit Tower, is the architectural structure perhaps most identified with our city after the Ferry Building and the bridges.

(Courtesy Wells Fargo Bank.)

The seal of the Vigilantes.

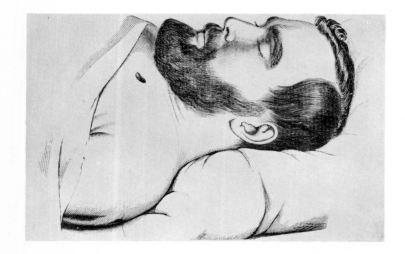

One of the Vigilantes' most famous victims was James P. Casey, who on May 14, 1856, shot down James King of William, editor of the San Francisco *Bulletin*. His unusual name distinguished him from another James King in the little town he had come from. (Courtesy California Historical Society.)

Montgomery Street in 1852, painted by
A. O. Dinsdale. (Courtesy Wells Fargo Bank.)

Execution of Hetherington and Brace. The two
murderers became victims of the Vigilantes' justice
on July 29, 1856. (Courtesy Wells Fargo Bank.)

About this time there commenced a parade of colorful characters peculiar to San Francisco which has never quite ended. There was, for example, the Great Unknown, who spoke to no one; "George Washington" Coombs, who knew he was the first President and became irritated at those who didn't; "the Guttersnipe," a ubiquitous beggar; Oofty Goofty, the wild man, who invited anyone to hit him for ten cents—until John L. Sullivan fractured his spine; Big Bertha, Queen of the Confidence Gals, who took to the stage once and made an exit strapped to the back of a donkey which fell into the orchestra pit.

There were the notorious criminals, such as Shanghai Kelley, who slugged or doped his victims in his saloon and shipped them off to sea. There were the great beauties and actresses: Adah Menken, Elisa Biscaccianti, Kitty Hayes, Lola Montez, and Lotta Crabtree, who drove such luminaries as Mark Twain, Bret Harte, and Joaquin Miller out of their literary minds.

There was the notorious madam Iodoform Kate, who operated along what is now Maiden Lane, and reputedly got her kicks by snorts of that medicinal fluid, and Mammy Pleasant, the sinister and bizarre Negress whose career as a machinationist would make a dozen novels.

And the most fantastic and best-loved character of all, Joshua A. Norton. He was a prosperous merchant, but something went haywire in his make-up when his scheme to corner the rice market in 1854 collapsed. From that time on he proclaimed himself Emperor Norton, and, strolling regally around the city in a general's uniform, he would supervise his empire, nodding benignly to his subjects, issuing proclamations, and passing out fake money which the citizens delightedly honored.

One of his contemporaries, B. E. Lloyd, wrote in part:

Perhaps the most original and best sustained character that is met on the streets of San Francisco is that of "Emperor," adopted by Joshua Norton, an English Jew. To look upon him, knowing his early history in the city, one feels like exclaiming with Ophelia, "How great a mind is here o'erthrown!" . . .

Emperor Norton.

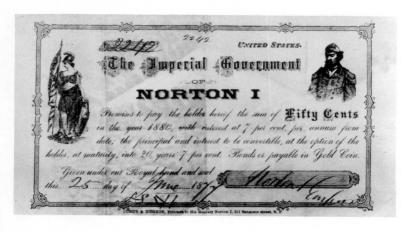

Two photos of Norton and a reproduction of the fake money he enjoyed handing out.
(Courtesy Wells Fargo Bank.)

He occasionally calls at the offices or business houses of acquaintances, stops for a few minutes, talking on general topics, and proceeds on his round—never calling at one place so often as to render his presence offensive, nor remaining so long as to be considered a bore. He is a good conversationalist, and having free access to all the libraries and reading rooms, keeps well posted on current topics. He will talk readily upon any subject, and his opinions are usually very correct, except when relating to himself. He is more familiar with history than the average citizen, and his scientific knowledge, though sometimes "mixed," is considerable. Of evenings he may be found at the theater or in the lecture room, a cool observer and attentive listener. His face is a free ticket for him to all places of amusement and public gatherings, and oftentimes he makes quite extended journeys by rail and other public conveyances without expending a dollar. Sacramento is a favorite resort during the sessions of the Legislature whither he goes to see that legislators do not prostitute their privileges. He is on familiar terms with all officials, high or low, feeling of course that they are only his more favored subjects. He is perfectly harmless, and unless his mind be occupied with some more than ordinarily grave question relating to the Empire, is jocular, and disposed to be humorous.

Upon the death of the two mongrels, Bummer and Lazarus, who accompanied him on his rounds for a decade, thousands of people attended their funeral. Norton was wont to communicate with Queen Victoria and the Czar of Russia, he enjoyed free rides on all trains and ferries, and he received new uniforms from the city whenever needed. After he died in 1880, ten thousand San Franciscans attended his funeral.

21

Stagecoach passing Mount Shasta. The painting was done by Aaron Stein, an executive of the Wells Fargo Company at the time.

The list of characters goes on and on. But despite the weird and sensational, despite the tales of wildness, the duels, the shanghaiing, and the wicked Barbary Coast, where in some cafés completely nude waitresses served the customers, a high percentage of San Franciscans were college graduates who came from well-established eastern families. Around the mid-1850s more respectable women began arriving in town. They rode around in handsome hacks, wearing their fashionable bloomers and satins in spite of the still muddy, unpaved streets. Already there were 150 bona-fide lawyers, there was an Opera House, there was the fashionable Pacific Club (now the Pacific Union Club on Nob Hill), and the nucleus of Mills College across the bay. Culture, in a polite-society sort of way, was growing. The first fashionable country residences were built "down the peninsula" (the area about twenty miles below today's San Francisco, encompassing San Mateo, Burlingame, Hillsborough and Woodside, Atherton and Palo Alto).

A good part of this interest in culture is owed to "the forty-eighters." Many liberal Europeans fled from the political unrest of that year, and to avoid prison sentences they came around the Horn to San Francisco just before the Gold Rush. It helps to explain why the first circulating libraries in the city featured books in many languages and why the city soon was supporting the finest in music and drama.

In 1859, while the East was working itself up to the Civil War, the West plunged itself into another rush for wealth. Silver was found in great shiny hunks totaling some $250,000,000 in the Washoe Silver Mines. This was the famous Comstock lode, which made the fortunes of such men as William Sharon, William Ralston, Adolph Sutro, John W. Mackay, James Flood, William O'Brien, "Lucky" Baldwin, George Hearst, and James G. Fair.

The 1860s marked the time of the West's being united with the East. On April 14, 1860, the first Pony Express rider arrived in San Francisco from St. Joseph, Missouri. A stamp for a half-ounce letter carried by him cost $5.

The Wells Fargo Company is an exciting name always associated with San Francisco. The company was founded in 1852 at 114 Montgomery Street as an express and banking business to serve the bustling phenomenon that Gold Rush California had become. The principal function of the company was to transport passengers and gold, and bank the latter at its destination. Using the Concord coach, which carried sixteen persons as well as mail and bullion, they made the trip from St. Joseph to San Francisco in sixteen days. And horrendous days they could be, what with the bad roads and the bandits.

The most famous of the highwaymen was Black Bart, who robbed twenty-eight stages single-handed. To add insult to injury, he usually left mocking, unnerving verses at the scene of each crime. There are many apocryphal verses ascribed to Black Bart but the lines printed below are genuine:

Black Bart.

here I lay me down to Sleep
to wait the coming morrow
perhaps Success, perhaps defeat
And everlasting sorrow.
I've labored long and hard for bread
for honor and for riches
But on my corns too long you've tread
You fine haired Sons of bitches.

Black Bart signed it "The PO 8," which was his little joke for "The poet."

After a decade of successful highwaymanship he was finally captured in 1883 by a Wells Fargo detective through a laundry mark on his handkerchief. Upon Bart's release from prison in 1888 Ambrose Bierce wrote a long poem in the San Francisco *Examiner*, one verse of which was:

> What's that?—you "ne'er again will rob a stage"?
> What! did you so? Faith, I didn't know it,
> Was *that* what threw poor Themis in a rage?
> I thought you were convicted as a poet.

The joining of the East with the West. The Golden Spike ceremony, 1869. Below is a photo of the original Golden Spike. (Photos: Union Pacific Railroad.)

In 1869 the Big Four—Charles Crocker, Collis Potter Huntington, Leland Stanford, and Mark Hopkins—connected their Central Pacific Railroad with the Union Pacific Railroad in Utah. The city's newspaper headlines blasted arrogantly, "San Francisco annexes the United States!"

In her book Julia Altrocchi says of San Francisco, "The Bonanza excitement was increasing rather than diminishing in San Francisco . . . except that this time you did not carry a pick and shovel to the quartz ledges . . . but you entered the Stock Exchange, laid down as many dollars as you could afford on Ophir or Belcher or some other recommended mine, and in a few hours you might be a Croesus or wiped out."

The wealthy Bonanza Kings and the Big Four began an orgy of building. Colton, Ben Ali Haggin, Tobin, Towne, Flood, Stanford, Hopkins, and Crocker were among the first names to build fantastic Victorian mansions on Nob Hill. Crocker spent $2,000,000 on his place and built a forty-foot "spite fence" around the property of an undertaker named Yung when he wouldn't sell out. The most dreadful private edifice was Mark Hopkins', of which Gertrude Atherton said, "It looked as if several architects had been employed and that they had fought one another to the finish."

In 1875 William Ralston built one of the most ornate and splendid hostelries of the world, "the Palace," which covered two and a half acres of land with a grand court in the center into which carriages could be driven (now covered over with glass and used as

24

a dining room). Writing of the Palace in 1876, B. E. Lloyd declared it a complete city unto itself and added, "There are also 437 bath tubs, which is an important consideration."

Besides the railroads, there were such lucrative enterprises as the Occidental and Oriental Steamship Company, the Pacific Mail steamers, and the great Bank of California, presided over by the shrewd Darius Ogden Mills.

For the next three decades San Franciscans pursued the things that money can buy with sybaritic zeal.

Lucius Beebe and Charles Clegg, in their *Cable Car Carnival*, say:

It was a decade of parquetry and marquetry, of baronial architecture and twenty-course public banquets, of solid gold table service and private ballrooms, of diamond stomachers and tiaras, of silver-mounted harnesses and solid gold doorknobs, of Prince Albert frock coats, of landaus and opera coaches and seagoing public hacks at every porte-cochere, of Adah Isaacs Menken in "Mazeppa," of Silver Palace sleeping cars on the overnight run from Vallejo to Virginia City, of Inverness cloaks, terrapin for luncheon, champagne for breakfast and the best vintage claret and Rainwater Madeira and Bourbon County whiskey at all times of day and night. Perhaps the imperial Romans in their fullest triumph of conquest, living off the plunder of a hundred provinces and the carefully skimmed cream of the known world, existed in a farrago of more luxurious devisings but none of San Francisco's McAllisters, Verdiers, Crockers and Haywards would have admitted it for a moment.

25

(Courtesy Pioneer Society.)

The insides of two very different houses of the period. The one above shows the interior of the old Rudolph Spreckels mansion at Clay and Van Ness Avenue, and the one below is the interior of the notorious Madam Tessie Wall's house, which never came close to being a home.

(Courtesy California Historical Society.)

The pre-fire Palace Hotel courtyard before it was converted into the dining room shown on page 67. (Photo: Moulin Studios.)

The old Tivoli Theater. (Courtesy Pioneer Society.)

An unusual type of photo for those days, this 1877 candid shot shows a family out for a stroll at Bush and Kearny Streets. The California Theater is in the background. (Courtesy California Historical Society.)

It was a gay, gaudy life—"the heyday of the theaters." It was said that at the time there were more theaters in San Francisco than in any city in the United States. A favorite was the Tivoli (see photo), where customers were served beer. Sarah Bernhardt, Tetrazzini, Edwin Booth, James O'Neill, Lily Langtry, and Lotta Crabtree (the "adorable hoyden") graced the stages. Isadora Duncan began teaching her "modern" dance, and the literati welcomed Robert Louis Stevenson, Gelett (Purple Cow) Burgess, Ambrose Bierce, Gertrude Atherton, and the short-lived Frank Norris (*McTeague* and *The Octopus*). And there were the famous painter William Keith and the great photographer Arnold Genthe, one of the earliest to practice "candid" photography.

More fashionable clubs were organized, among them the Bohemian Club and the Burlingame Country Club. Del Monte Lodge was constructed by Charles Crocker to build up the week-end business on his railroad into a social event.

Leland Stanford started building his university in Palo Alto. William Hammond Hall, aided by John McLaren, reclaimed the wastes of the sand dunes and made them into Golden Gate Park, where a large Mid-Winter Fair was held to advertise the beauties and climate of the coast. (It rained!)

San Francisco restaurants became famous not only for their "naughty rooms upstairs for mashers," but for their fine food and original recipes. John C. Kirkpatrick, of the Palace Hotel, first thought of baking bivalves in the half-shell with a highly seasoned tomato sauce, and thus created the famous oysters Kirkpatrick. Crab legs meunière, Olympia oyster cocktail, and chop suey were said to have been first introduced in San Francisco. Among the famous old restaurants were the Poodle Dog (founded in 1849 and still going strong), Maison Doré, and Marchand's, and people used to go there "to see the elephant" (as San Franciscans referred to painting the town red).

Popular North Beach restaurants were Sanguinetti's, Pappa Coppa's, and Luna's.

Sundays were spent riding out to the Cliff House on bicycles, or wandering through the fabulous Woodward Gardens, or racing four-in-hand coaches along the Great Highway. The Ned Greenway Cotillions were begun. Life began to become more international. Princess Louise, Queen Victoria's daughter, visited us, Flora Sharon married Lord Fermor-Hesketh of England, and Beth Sperry married Prince Poniatowski of Poland.

One shouldn't think that with all this elegance the city had abandoned its coarser forms of amusement. As late as 1876 Lloyd, in *Lights and Shades*, described "the curse mark on San Francisco's brow" thus:

Almost nightly there are drunken carousals and broils, frequently terminating in dangerous violence. Men are often garroted and robbed, and it is not by any means a rare occurrence for foul murder to be committed. "Murderers' Corner" and "Deadman's Alley" have been re-baptized with blood over and over again, and yet call for other sacrifices. Barbary Coast is the haunt of the low and vile of every kind. The petty thief, the house burglar, the tramp, the whore-monger, lewd women, cut-throats and murderers, are all found there. Dance-houses and Concert saloons, where blear-eyed men and faded women drink vile liquor, smoke offensive tobacco,

The bawdy, the infamous "Terrific Street"—the Barbary Coast. (Courtesy California Historical Society.)

engage in vulgar conduct, sing obscene songs, and say and do everything to heap upon themselves more degradation, unrest and misery, are numerous. Low gambling houses thronged with riot-loving rowdies in all stages of intoxication are there. Opium dens where heathen Chinese and God-forsaken women and men are sprawled in miscellaneous confusion, disgustingly drowsy, or completely overcome by inhaling the vapors of the nauseous narcotic, are there. Licentiousness, debauchery, pollution, loathsome disease, insanity from dissipation, misery, poverty, wealth, profanity, blasphemy and death, are there. And Hell, yawning to receive the putrid mass, is there also.

What a happy, graphic phrase is "sprawled in miscellaneous confusion"!

The most dramatic three days in San Francisco's history came in 1906. The city had had earthquakes before. Early Spanish records speak of them and there is an account of a violent quake in 1812, another one in 1865, and a highly damaging one in 1868.

"Familiarity with danger subdues fear and dread," B. E. Lloyd had written in 1876, "and a year's residence in San Francisco will quiet any fearful apprehensions from earthquakes. While it would not be very strange if a shock should visit San Francisco, so powerful as to lay much of the city in ruins, and consequently be very destructive to life, yet it is not probable that such an event will transpire. And, even if it should, the disastrous result would not be greater than attends the scourges from epidemic diseases that so often prevail in Eastern cities, from which San Francisco is almost wholly exempt. 'Every place has its drawbacks,' said the old farmer after a day's havoc among the Canada thistles that had overrun his farm; 'Jones, whose quarter-section joins mine on the right has to fight fox-tail, and Brown, just below my paster there, has chinch-bugs in his corn,

Looking up Powell Street from Sutter in the middle 1890s, with the Stanford and Hopkins mansions at the top of Nob Hill. (Photo: Moulin Studios.)

This superb picture, taken by a Berkeley photographer named Lange, shows the Broadway wharf in the 1890s. (Courtesy San Francisco Maritime Museum.)

and his small grain is all a-rustin'—so we has to put up with our little dif-*fick*-ulties.' California has its earthquakes—"

When our little dif-*fick*-ulty came, it was a beaut, and no mistake. On April 18, 1906, a little after five a.m., the entire city began to tremble and shake. There was a terrible noise, "like the roar of 10,000 lions," and San Franciscans knew they were in the center of a nightmarish earthquake. Cable cars jerked to a stop and the $7,000,000 City Hall crumbled like a movie set. The glass roof over the Palace Hotel court splintered and

The Call=Chronicle=Examiner

SAN FRANCISCO, THURSDAY, APRIL 19, 1906.

EARTHQUAKE AND FIRE: SAN FRANCISCO IN RUINS

DEATH AND DESTRUCTION HAVE BEEN THE FATE OF SAN FRANCISCO. SHAKEN BY A TEMBLOR AT 5:13 O'CLOCK YESTERDAY MORNING, THE SHOCK LASTING 48 SECONDS, AND SCOURGED BY FLAMES THAT RAGED DIAMETRICALLY IN ALL DIRECTIONS, THE CITY IS A MASS OF SMOULDERING RUINS. AT SIX O'CLOCK LAST EVENING THE FLAMES SEEMINGLY PLAYING WITH INCREASED VIGOR, THREATENED TO DESTROY SUCH SECTIONS AS THEIR FURY HAD SPARED DURING THE EARLIER PORTION OF THE DAY. BUILDING THEIR PATH IN A TRIANGUAR CIRCUIT FROM THE START IN THE EARLY MORNING, THEY JOCKEYED AS THE DAY WANED, LEFT THE BUSINESS SECTION, WHICH THEY HAD ENTIRELY DEVASTATED, AND SKIPPED IN A DOZEN DIRECTIONS TO THE RESIDENCE PORTIONS. AS NIGHT FELL THEY HAD MADE THEIR WAY OVER INTO THE NORTH BEACH SECTION AND SPRINGING ANEW AS THEY REACHED OUT ALONG THE SHIPPING SECTION DOWN THE BAY SHORE, OVER THE HILLS AND ACROSS TOWARD THIRD AND TOWNSEND STREETS. WAREHOUSES, WHOLESALE HOUSES AND MANUFACTURING CONCERNS FELL IN THEIR PATH. THIS COMPLETED THE DESTRUCTION OF THE ENTIRE DISTRICT KNOWN AS THE "SOUTH OF MARKET STREET." HOW FAR THEY ARE REACHING TO THE SOUTH ACROSS THE CHANNEL CANNOT BE TOLD AS THIS PART OF THE CITY IS SHUT OFF FROM SAN FRANCISCO PAPERS.

AFTER DARKNESS, THOUSANDS OF THE HOMELESS WERE MAKING THEIR WAY WITH THEIR BLANKETS AND SCANT PROVISIONS TO GOLDEN GATE PARK AND THE BEACH TO FIND SHELTER. THOSE IN THE HOMES ON THE HILLS JUST NORTH OF THE HAYES VALLEY WRECKED SECTION PILED THEIR BELONGINGS IN THE STREETS AND EXPRESS WAGONS AND AUTOMOBILES WERE HAULING THE THINGS AWAY TO THE SPARSELY SETTLED REGIONS. EVERYBODY IN SAN FRANCISCO IS PREPARED TO LEAVE THE CITY, FOR THE BELIEF IS FIRM THAT SAN FRANCISCO WILL BE TOTALLY DESTROYED.

DOWNTOWN EVERYTHING IS RUIN. NOT A BUSINESS HOUSE STANDS. THEATRES ARE CRUMBLED INTO HEAPS. FACTORIES AND COMMISSION HOUSES LIE SMOULDERING ON THEIR FORMER SITES. ALL OF THE NEWSPAPER PLANTS HAVE BEEN RENDERED USELESS, THE "CALL" AND THE "EXAMINER" BUILDINGS, EXCLUDING THE "CALL'S" EDITORIAL ROOMS ON STEVENSON STREET BEING ENTIRELY DESTROYED.

IT IS ESTIMATED THAT THE LOSS IN SAN FRANCISCO WILL REACH FROM $150,000,000 TO $200,000,000. THESE FIGURES ARE IN THE ROUGH AND NOTHING CAN BE TOLD UNTIL PARTIAL ACCOUNTING IS TAKEN.

ON EVERY SIDE THERE WAS DEATH AND SUFFERING YESTERDAY. HUNDREDS WERE INJURED, EITHER BURNED, CRUSHED OR STRUCK BY FALLING PIECES FROM THE BUILDINGS AND ONE OF TEN DIED WHILE ON THE OPERATING TABLE AT MECHANICS' PAVILION IMPROVISED AS A HOSPITAL FOR THE COMFORT AND CARE OF 300 OF THE INJURED. THE NUMBER OF DEAD IS NOT KNOWN BUT IT IS ESTIMATED THAT AT LEAST 500 MET THEIR DEATH IN THE HORROR.

AT NINE O'CLOCK, UNDER A SPECIAL MESSAGE FROM PRESIDENT ROOSEVELT, THE CITY WAS PLACED UNDER MARTIAL LAW. HUNDREDS OF TROOPS PATROLLED THE STREETS AND DROVE THE CROWDS BACK, WHILE HUNDREDS MORE WERE SET AT WORK ASSISTING THE FIRE AND POLICE DEPARTMENTS. THE STRICTEST ORDERS WERE ISSUED, AND IN TRUE MILITARY SPIRIT THE SOLDIERS OBEYED. DURING THE AFTERNOON THREE THIEVES MET THEIR DEATH BY RIFLE BULLETS WHILE AT WORK IN THE RUINS. THE CURIOUS WERE DRIVEN BACK AT THE BREASTS OF THE HORSES THAT THE CAVALRYMEN RODE AND ALL THE CROWDS WERE FORCED FROM THE LEVEL DISTRICT TO THE HILLY SECTION BEYOND TO THE NORTH.

THE WATER SUPPLY WAS ENTIRELY CUT OFF, AND MAY BE IT WAS JUST AS WELL, FOR THE LINES OF FIRE DEPARTMENT WOULD HAVE BEEN ABSOLUTELY USELESS AT ANY STAGE. ASSISTANT CHIEF DOUGHERTY SUPERVISED THE WORK OF HIS MEN AND EARLY IN THE MORNING IT WAS SEEN THAT THE ONLY POSSIBLE CHANCE TO SAVE THE CITY LAY IN EFFORT TO CHECK THE FLAMES BY THE USE OF DYNAMITE. DURING THE DAY A BLAST COULD BE HEARD IN ANY SECTION AT INTERVALS OF ONLY A FEW MINUTES, AND BUILDINGS NOT DESTROYED BY FIRE WERE BLOWN TO ATOMS. BUT THROUGH THE GAPS MADE THE FLAMES JUMPED AND ALTHOUGH THE FAILURES OF THE HEROIC EFFORTS OF THE POLICE FIREMEN AND SOLDIERS WERE AT TIMES SICKENING, THE WORK WAS CONTINUED WITH A DESPERATION THAT WILL LIVE AS ONE OF THE FEATURES OF THE TERRIBLE DISASTER. MEN WORKED LIKE FIENDS TO COMBAT THE LAUGHING, ROARING, ONRUSHING FIRE DEMON.

NO HOPE LEFT FOR SAFETY OF ANY BUILDINGS

San Francisco seems doomed to entire destruction. With a lapse in the raging of the flames just before dark, the hope was raised that with the use of the tons of dynamite the course of the fire might be checked and confined to the triangular sections it had cut out for its path. But on the Barbary Coast the fire broke out anew and as night closed in the flames were eating their way into parts untouched in their ravages during the day. To the south and the north they spread; down to the docks and out into the resident section, in and to the north of Hayes Valley. By six o'clock practically all of St. Ignatius' great buildings were no more. They had been leveled to the fiery heap that marked what was once the metropolis of the West.

The first of the big structures to go to ruin was the Call Building, the famous skyscraper. At eleven o'clock the big 18-story building was a furnace. Flames leaped from every window and shot skyward from the circular windows in the dome. In less than two hours nothing remained but the tall skeleton.

By five o'clock the Palace Hotel was in ruins. The old hostelry, famous the world over, withstood the siege until the last and although dynamite was used in frequent blasts to drive

Continued on Page Two

BLOW BUILDINGS UP TO CHECK FLAMES

The dynamiting of buildings in the track of the fire, to stay the progress of the flames, was in charge of John Bermingham, Jr., superintendent of the California Powder Works. Several experienced men from the powder works, assisted by policemen and members of the fire department, did the hazardous work of blowing up the buildings. They were raised in sets of threes, but the open spaces where the shattered buildings fell were quickly turned into holocausts of flame. The work was most effective in the business blocks east of Kearny street.

WHOLE CITY IS ABLAZE

At 10 o'clock last night the Occidental Hotel was destroyed by the flames which swept on, reached across Montgomery street and attacked the block bounded by Montgomery, Sutter, Bush and Kearny. The new Merchants' Exchange building was a mass of flames from basement to tower.

The Union Trust building and Crocker-Woolworth B ck were both ablaze and the Chronicle building and other buildings in that block were threatened by the flames.

Shortly after 10 o'clock the fire had eaten its way southward from Portsmouth Square to Kearny and California streets. The entire section fronting on the west side of Kearny street was doomed.

All the buildings adjoining the Hall of Justice on the residence section as far as Gough street. There, by dynamiting blocks after blocks, the firemen succeeded in checking the devouring element.

CHURCH OF SAINT IGNATIUS IS DESTROYED

The magnificent church and College of St. Ignatius, on the northwest corner of Van Ness avenue and Hayes street represents in its destruction a material loss of over $1,000,000. The actual cost of the great building was over $900,000, but during the years which have elapsed since its erection the church has been enriched by paintings and frescoes, which were priceless. Some of them were works of art which can never be replaced, however willing those interested in the church might be to meet any expense in the effort.

MAYOR CONFERS WITH MILITARY AND CITIZENS

At 1 o'clock yesterday afternoon 50 representative citizens of San Francisco met the Mayor, the Chief of Police and the United States Military authorities in the police office in the basement of the Hall of Justice. They had been summoned thither by Mayor Schmitz early in the forenoon, the fearful possibilities of the situation having forced themselves upon him immediately after the shock of earthquake in the morning, and the news which at once reached him of the completeness of the diaster. He lost no time in making out a list of citizens from whom to seek advice and assistance, and in summoning them to the conference. It was called at the Hall of Justice, as virtually the first news which reached the Mayor regarding the extent of the disaster was that of the ruin of the City Hall. He did not realize that even while the conference was to be going on cornices would be crashing down and windows falling in fragments in the Hall of Justice also, and that before sunset desperate efforts would be made to blow the structure up in the vain endeavor by this means to check the advance of the flames in the northern section of the downtown district.

All, or nearly all of the citizens summoned to the conference

Continued on Page Two

rained down glass, while Enrico Caruso rushed out onto Market Street, a towel around his famous throat, clutching an autographed photo of Theodore Roosevelt. He collected himself enough finally to sing at the top of his lungs to be sure his vocal chords had not been injured. "Give me Vesuvius!" he said, and left the city forever.

San Franciscans insist on telling one, "It wasn't an earthquake that destroyed us, it was the Fire." Starting in the business section down near Montgomery Street and "South of Market" district, the giant flames swept toward Russian Hill, Chinatown, North Beach, and Telegraph Hill.

This extraordinarily fine photo was made by Arnold Genthe with a camera snatched from a photographic store when his own studio burned. It was taken from Powell Street looking down Sacramento. (Courtesy California Historical Society.)

The three newspapers banded together to produce this extra the day after the quake.

The burning city. (From a painting by W. A. Coulter.)

Market Street aflame. (Courtesy Wells Fargo Bank.)

Opposite: One could say that these young ladies had not quite appreciated the extent of the tragedy being enacted behind them when Arnold Genthe snapped this photo. (Courtesy Palace of the Legion of Honor.)

On Nob Hill Gertrude Atherton saw the Fairmont as it burned. "The new marble hotel on the highest hill poured up volumes of white smoke from the top alone while the hundreds of windows were like plates of brass."

Jack London looked down California Street and saw "two mighty walls of fire advancing from the east and south."

The water mains broke, the gasworks blew up, and the chief of the Fire Department perished when the chimney of his home fell on him as he slept in bed. By mid-morning the Fire Department resorted to dynamiting the downtown business district to stop the flaming fury which was being blown rapidly by a west wind, obliterating everything in its path. In a few short hours most of San Francisco was in ruins.

Wonderful tales have come out of these horrendous hours. John Barrymore, having just wobbled home from a party, was jostled from his hotel couch and when he fled to the street was impressed by militia men to help with the rescue efforts. When sister Ethel, upon receiving a cable to this effect, asked John Drew if he thought it was true, he replied, "Quite probably, but it took an act of God to get the fellow out of bed and the U.S. Army to get him to work!"

A. P. Giannini saved all the cash in the Bank of Italy (now the richest bank in the world, the Bank of America) by hauling it off in a vegetable cart to his home on the Peninsula.

Several houses were saved on Telegraph Hill by the Italians pouring wine on the flames.

A servant of the W. H. Crockers grabbed a painting off the wall as the blaze curled around him and ran to safety—with Millet's famous "Man with a Hoe."

The homeless took refuge in the Presidio, Richmond District, and Golden Gate Park. Tents were set up, then outdoor kitchens, and a makeshift operating room, where several

Another Genthe photo showing the emergency conditions following the fire. It destroyed the newly built City Hall, seen in ruins in the background. Of interest to photography enthusiasts is the fact that the great modern master Ansel Adams made this print from old Genthe negatives. (Courtesy Palace of the Legion of Honor.)

babies were born. The city was placed under martial law and soldiers were given orders to shoot pillagers on sight. The number of dead for the first day was estimated at 500 out of a population of around 342,000.

But the city was far from beaten. Henry Miller, a millionaire cattle rancher, gave out free beef to the homeless for seven days, and merchant Raphael Weill imported trainloads of clothes and personally walked through the tent cities to see that everyone was clothed. A writer of the day proclaimed, "The few blocks that have been destroyed were not San Francisco. They were just buildings!"

The citizens' feelings were expressed in the much-quoted poem of Lawrence W. Harris:

> From the Ferry to Van Ness you're a
>   God-forsaken mess,
> But the damnedest, finest ruins, nothing more
>   and nothing less.

Dramatically it would be pleasing to think that the woman in this heretofore unpublished photo was crying for a lost city, but in all probability it is the stench along Dupont Street (Grant Avenue now) from broken sewers and trapped Chinese bodies that has produced the handkerchief. Four-fifths of San Francisco had been destroyed, between 450 and 500 people killed, 1500 injured, and 250,000 made homeless. (Courtesy California Historical Society.)

San Franciscans set to with a will. Big billboards appeared around town saying, "Don't talk earthquake—talk business."

By 1909 the city was almost completely rebuilt at a cost of $150,000,000 to the city and $225,000,000 to fire-insurance companies.

San Francisco cleared away not only the ruins of the fallen City Hall but the human rubble that had been in it, for the graft and corruption had reached heroic—if that's the word—proportions. Rudolph Spreckels financed an investigation of the appalling conditions to the tune of $100,000, and was aided by his friend James Phelan and Fremont Older, editor of the *Call Bulletin,* who dedicated his newspaper to a crusade against the underworld. The rodents to be fumigated turned out to be Mayor Schmitz himself and his sly cohort, Abe Ruef. Prosecution was difficult because of lack of witnesses, who quite rightly feared for their lives if they testified. The trials were the most explosive ever held in San Francisco, with the house of the chief witness being dynamited, prosecuting attorney Francis J. Heney shot in the jaw, and Fremont Older himself was kidnaped. The upshot was that in 1907 Schmitz was sentenced to San Quentin for five years, and in 1908 Ruef was convicted on 129 counts of civic graft and sentenced to a fourteen-year term.

Within the decade the Civic Center was constructed, a lovely square sparkling with fountains surrounded by French- and Renaissance-style buildings such as City Hall, the Public Library, and the Civic Auditorium. Publisher Michael de Young gave the city the M. H. de Young Museum in the Golden Gate Park, and the Adolph Spreckelses gave the stately California Palace of the Legion of Honor overlooking the Golden Gate.

While the rest of the world was preparing for World War I San Francisco held a highly successful World's Fair—the Panama-Pacific International Exposition, celebrating the new boost to western commerce, the opening of the Panama Canal.

The next exposition, the Golden Gate Fair, was in 1939-1940, and the intervening years were good ones of calm progress. Then with World War II the town expanded and progress became and has remained more frenetic.

The United Nations was born here in 1945, and it was a new high for the city. Since then San Francisco has continued to build, to prosper, to burgeon, and while never losing sight of the past it looks steadily to the future.

Congratulations after the sensational trials of 1907. From left to right: W. J. Burns, Fremont Older (who was kidnaped), Mrs. Older, Francis J. Heney (prosecuting attorney who was shot), Charles W. Cobb, and Rudolph B. Spreckels, who financed the investigation. (Courtesy California Historical Society.)

The second of a series of several Cliff Houses in a splendid photo taken in 1906, the year before it burned. For well over half a century San Franciscans have enjoyed watching the seals from this spectacular restaurant site. (Courtesy Moulin Studios.)

The 1939 Golden Gate Exposition was held on Treasure Island, the largest man-made island in the world. The photo shows the Palace of Homes and Gardens. (Courtesy San Francisco *Chronicle*.)

The once magnificent Palace of Fine Arts. It's more impressive at night, for then one can't see the chicken wire and laths and crumbling plaster. Created by Bernard Maybeck for the 1915 Panama Pacific International Exposition, it was inspired by Arnold Böcklin's painting, "The Isle of the Dead." It was built to last only one year, but after the exposition was over San Franciscans couldn't bear to destroy the beautiful structure. In May 1959 Walter S. Johnson, a former San Francisco newsboy who made his fortune in the lumber business, volunteered $2,000,000 for its preservation. (Photo: Bob Campbell.)

"This city never changes," someone remarked to me recently. Yet look at the photos on these pages. Taken in 1957 and 1958, they are already out of date.

The barkers for the girlie shows are silent along lower Pacific Street, for the historic Barbary Coast is no more; where moral people once used to point righteous forefingers and cry, "Sodom and Gomorrah," there now has appeared a row of chicly self-conscious decorators' shops.

A barker in the International Settlement. (Photo: John G. Roberts.)

The Embarcadero.

Mrs. Elinor Chatfield-Taylor takes her children for one of the last rides on the Bay ferry. Competition from the bridges finally made it uneconomic to run these boats. (Photo: Jerome Zerbe.)

The spirit of this city does not change, but the physical is another matter. Since this lovely panorama of the Embarcadero was taken, calamitous things have happened; the stately Ferry Building, copied from Seville's Giralda tower, has been truncated by a concrete slash of enslaving progress known—ironically—as a freeway. The ferry boat setting out resolutely for Oakland's shore was the last of its breed and will never make that wonderful trip again.

(Photo: Gene Wright.)

These photos show better than words the changes that have come in eighty-two years to "changeless" San Francisco.

Compare these two splendid panoramas and the changes wrought in a relatively short time. The top one was taken by pioneer photographer Eadweard Muybridge in 1877 and is a paste-up of several photos. It was taken from the Mark Hopkins Mansion and looks down California Street at the left. Notice that the Flood mansion hasn't been built yet,

that the Crocker Mansion (complete with spite fence) stands where Grace Cathedral is today, and that Telegraph Hill is Coitless.

The lower photo was taken in 1959 by Gene Wright's amazing wide-angle camera, from slightly higher up in the Mark Hokpins Hotel.

And, of course, the cast of characters changes. Where are those of only yesterday—and I mean yesterday, not yesteryear—those like Izzy Gomez, Tiny "Birdwhistle" Armstrong, Anita Zabala Howard Vanderbilt, Bill Saroyan, "Mom" Chung, Joe "Shreve" Foreman, Murphy Hirschberg, and Francis Van Wie, the nineteen-times-married Ding Dong Daddy of the D Line? If the Reaper doesn't summon them, New York and Malibu seem to.

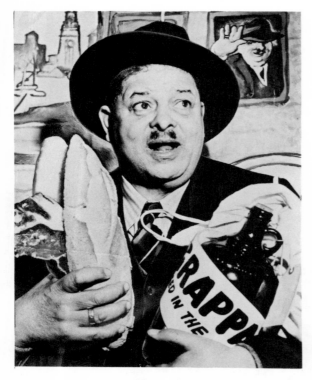

(Photo: San Francisco *Chronicle*.)

Izzy Gomez, whose place was more of a salon than a saloon.

William Saroyan, Pulitzer Prize winner, is still claimed by San Francisco though he has lived away for a decade. (Photo: San Francisco *Chronicle*.)

It's hard to define Tiny Armstrong, somehow. It seems a bit inconclusive simply to say he was a fat man who wandered around town in various costumes, blowing a bird whistle, but that about sums it up. (Photo: San Francisco *Chronicle*.)

Joe "Shreve" Foreman opens the door for Mrs. Michael Tobin and Gorham Knowles.

So San Francisco does change and is changing and this book can give a picture only of *today;* tomorrow will date other photographs in this book, perhaps even before it reaches the bookstores. There's nothing to be done but present the city and the people as I think of them right now, and hope that it will someday re-create for my children, fourth-generation San Franciscans themselves, the way it was in this era.

And what do I think of when I think of San Francisco *now?*

What images come to mind?

When I think of modern San Francisco, I think of many things. I think of . . .

Opposite: The San Francisco-Oakland Bay Bridge (better known as the Bay Bridge) and the downtown skyscrapers of the city in a view from Yerba Buena Island. The bridge, which stretches 8¼ miles across the Bay, was finished in November 1936, six months before the completion of the Golden Gate Bridge.

THE VIEWS

(Photo: Ewing Galloway.)

Though we pretend to be blasé about the Top of the Mark, a good many San Franciscans start an evening on the town with cocktails there, gaping at the wonderful view like any of the tourists. (Courtesy *Life* magazine.)

Looking toward Oakland and the Bay Bridge. (Photo: Jerome Zerbe.)

A clear day from the Top of the Mark. (Photo: Jerome Zerbe.)

View from Golden Gate Heights overlooking the Park and the
Presidio toward Marin County. (Photo: Bob Hollingsworth.)

A sea-gull's-eye view of San Francisco's forty-five-square-mile area. The uppermost bridge is the Golden Gate, leading northeast from the Presidio to Marin County. The lower bridge is the Bay Bridge, leading east to Oakland. In the upper left-hand corner you can see the white strip of Pacific waves pounding on the beach. (Photo: Clyde Sunderland.)

Treasure Island and Yerba Buena seen from Telegraph Hill. (Photo: Wes Pease.)

Opposite: As the sun quickly followed the rain, a fine shot from Russian Hill was taken. (Photo: Carolyn Mason Jones.)

Panorama view from Twin Peaks. (Photo: Ansel Adams. Courtesy American Trust Co.)

(Photo: Jacqueline Paul.)

THE FOG

I believe Carl Sandburg would find that the feet on which the fog of San Francisco comes are more those of a hefty cougar than of any cat.

But according to official statistics, the hours of fog over the San Francisco Bay itself average only 153 hours per year! Is it that ours, when it does come, is so much *foggier* that makes people think there are more days of it?

Night-club comedians have a field day with the fog, reveling in such remarks as "Woke up this morning to the coughing of the birds."

But actually, many San Franciscans, including myself, enjoy it when it comes. This isn't Pollyanna's "Glad Game"; we really like the feel, the smell, and the look of the city as the misty stuff enfolds it.

Joseph Henry Jackson wrote of it so well in his *My San Francisco* (New York: Crowell, 1953):

One warm afternoon everybody smiles; there is a cottony white line straight along the hilltops that separate downtown San Francisco from the westward sea slope. By five o'clock that white line will break; urged by the afternoon wind the fog will flow slowly over the ridge, filling the small canyons, pouring softly down the steep streets into town.

If the air currents happen that way, a long gray finger will move in through the Golden Gate and across to the East Bay where it widens at the shoreline, rising and mantling the hills

Fog over Alcatraz. (Photo: Betty Pollock.)

behind Berkeley and Oakland until next morning when the sun burns through the saturated air, sucking up the mists and dissolving them for another day. This is the summer sea fog for which the city is so widely known.

There is also the *tule* fog, so called by the Spaniards for the rushes in the river valleys of the Sacramento and the San Joaquin, a thick, low-lying river mist that forms during winter nights and drains toward the sea at the rate of about one mile an hour. Old San Francisco hands can tell it instantly by its musty, damp earth smell.

There is another low-lying fog, due to radiation cooling on winter nights; it hugs the land and vanishes before noon, burned away from the top down, lingering latest in the streets themselves.

The longer-lasting "high fog" is usually a mixture of smoke, dust, and vapor; it will form in the spring and fall, drift toward the sea as the morning advances, and return early in the afternoon, blown back by the west wind. The easterner would think of this change as a clouding over. It is the least beautiful of fogs, but the San Franciscan loves it too; he knows it for another aspect of the great ocean thermostat at work.

He knows also a familiar fact which the visitor is likely to find most curious of all. Weather, in the Bay region, is highly variable in space as well as in time. You may leave the city in the pleasant slanting sunlight of a June afternoon, on your way perhaps to the half-hidden suburban town of Ross at the foot of Mount Tamalpais to the north in Marin County. As you take the rising approach to the Golden Gate Bridge, a solid bank of fog almost hides the towers; you roll up the car window against the buffeting wind and the wetness on your left cheek; ahead you watch the fog spilling over the hills; moving silently down to Sausalito*

*Incidentally, it was originally, and correctly, spelled Saucelito, "Little Willow." [B.C.]

at the water's edge. Then you are across the Gate. You sweep through a short tunnel and between the high earth walls of a deep cut, and you are out again in flooding sunshine, warmer than you left in town. Three kinds of weather in ten minutes; a summer's day commonplace to the San Franciscan.

The city's weather is excellent, with a daily mean maximum temperature of 62.6 degrees causing a feeling of perpetual autumn. The sun shines in San Francisco 66 out of every 100 possible hours and the average annual rainfall is 20.5 inches.

While the rest of California swelters in the summer heat, San Francisco is cool; a familiar July sight is that of the poor shivering tourist walking along the street in a light Palm Beach suit which was so appropriate for the New York he just left.

San Franciscans like to attribute their women's beauty, in part, to two geographical facts: the fog and climate give them beautiful complexions, and climbing the hilly streets gives them trim legs. Whatever the reasons, the city's women are attractive and chic. One frequently hears it said that the San Francisco secretary is the best-dressed class of woman in the world, and a simple walk down Montgomery Street or around Union Square corroborates this statement.

Summer fog.

(Photo:
Mason Weymouth.)

The Ferry Building.

(Photo: Gene Wright.)

Although we are proud of our copper-domed City Hall, which is just a shade less tall than the nation's Capitol, the late Frank Lloyd Wright turned from it in disgust, muttering, "It's time you had another earthquake here!" (Photo: Wes Pease.)

THE ARCHITECTURE

The Ferry Building, stalwart symbol of the city since 1898, lasted through the earthquake.

The first regular ferry boat, the *Kangaroo*, ran from San Francisco to San Antonio Creek, now the Oakland Estuary. In the 1920s and 1930s, the *Delta King* and *Delta Queen* made overnight trips up the Sacramento River. Dubbed "the Mr. and Mrs. Smith Line" because of the number of illicit couples who patronized it of a week end, it featured music, good food, and dancing.

The high point of the ferry era was in 1930, when there were fifty-nine of them on the bay. But eventually, with the coming of the bridges, they were pronounced uneconomical, an unforgivable sin in our culture. In 1958, the last ferry, the *Piedmont*, made the final sad run decked in black, and it was the end of an era.

One can find all types of architecture in this city, from the Moorish Ferry Building and the Louis XIV-style City Hall, and Italian Renaissance St. Francis Hotel, to the Stock Exchange, which features Ralph Stackpole's statues symbolizing "Mother Earth's fruitfulness and man's inventive genius."

Behind this fountain in Huntington Park the Pacific Union Club is seen at left and the Mark Hopkins Hotel in the background at right. The club was built by James Flood in 1882 at a cost of $1,500,000, and he had one servant who did nothing but shine its $30,000 brass fence so that it "would flash for the entire length of two blocks." Flood, formerly a co-proprietor of the Auction Lunch Saloon, ended up as one of the more flamboyant of the silver bonanza kings. (Photo: Conrad.)

Opposite: Lunch or dinner is always a chic occasion in the elegant Garden Palm Court of the old Palace Hotel. Compare this photograph with the pre-earthquake—excuse me, pre-fire—one on page 27. The original Palace was built in 1875, at a cost of $5,000,000, principally by William Ralston, an Ohioan who had made a fortune in mining stocks and banking.

In San Francisco, the East mixes with the West in architectural styles as well as cooking. Here geisha-style waitresses serve *sushi* (raw fish) and *sake* (rice wine) at the Tokyo Sukiyaki on Fisherman's Wharf. In keeping with Japanese tradition, guests are invited to remove their shoes as they enter, and to kneel at the low tables for their meal. (Photo: *Life*.)

(Photo: Conrad.)

This modern, light-flooded building, surrounded by acres of lawn, is the Fireman Fund building. With 675 insurance carriers, agents, and brokers, San Francisco is the insurance hub of the West, as well as the financial center. An impressive portion of the world's finance is controlled from our Wall Street—Montgomery Street. San Francisco is the home of seven of the nation's hundred largest banks, including the world's largest, and is headquarters for the Twelfth Federal Reserve District, which is ranked third in volume of business measured by bank debits. Food processing is one of the city's largest industries; printing and publishing, apparel, fabricated metals, machinery, and chemical products are also produced in great volume.

Another of our most modern buildings is the windowless V. C. Morris china and glass-ware shop on Maiden Lane built in 1948 by the late Frank Lloyd Wright. (Photo: Conrad.)

In the foreground is the famous Mission Dolores (more correctly called Mission San Francisco de Asís) which was founded in June 1776 by Father Junípero Serra, five days before the Declaration of Independence. The present building was begun in 1782, and its four-foot-thick adobe walls were damaged but not destroyed by the earthquake. The tiles on the roof are also original. In the graveyard lie the remains of many historical figures, including those of James P. Casey (see page 18). The baroque church next to it is Spanish Colonial in style, but comparatively recent. (Photo: Art Frisch.)

In the heart of the business district is the Stock Exchange, at left, with Ralph Stackpole's modern sculptured figures; and the Royal Insurance building at right, with the lion and unicorn clock over the entrance. (Photo: Bob Hollingsworth.)

Look at the variety of architecture in this scant block and a half of California Street. Such a close juxtaposition of so many styles would be hard to find any place else in the world. (Photo: Conrad.)

(Photo: Gene Wright.)

Surrounded by the formal French garden, City Hall is one of the eight municipal and Federal buildings comprised in the Civic Center, just off Market Street.

The Temple Emanu-El. (Photo: Conrad.)

The Temple Emanu-El is the city's center of Reform Judaism. Romanesque, it was designed by the architects Schnaittacker, Bakewell, and Brown. The Jewish families in San Francisco, often from pioneer origins, include some of the most prominent and active people in the city's life and development. And this has always been so. For example, here is what the historian Lloyd wrote way back in 1876:

The Jews are numerous in San Francisco. A fair estimate places the number at twenty thousand. As citizens, they are very valuable to the community. There is not that hard line of distinction between them and the Christian population that is so generally apparent elsewhere. In California, Catholic and Protestant, Jew and Gentile, all seem to have united in the one effort of establishing a civilization on a broad and liberal foundation, the rules of which would not restrict in any way the liberties of any, so long as they observed the acknowledged principles of right. There is a more liberal religious sentiment among all sects in San Francisco than obtains in most American cities. It is a noteworthy fact that there are a less number of Jews arraigned before the criminal tribunals of the city than any other class of citizens. In no instance has a Jew been before the courts of San Francisco to answer for the crime of Murder.

The Sentinel building was built shortly after the disaster of 1906. It was the brain child of political boss Abe Ruef, and after serving as his headquarters played host to numberless artists and writers. This was also the birthplace of the Caesar salad—Caesar's Grill was in the basement. The building has been redecorated and rechristened Columbus Towers. (Photo: Bob Hollingsworth.)

Next page: The imposing doorway of the William Sproule mansion on Nob Hill at Sacramento and Taylor seems incongruously old-world on fashionable Nob Hill. (Photo: Ione Hyman.)

(Photo: Miriam Young.)

It takes a long arm to reach the bell at some doorways.

78

Another typically elegant doorway—belonging to the Robert Watt Miller residence on Nob Hill. (Photo: Ione Hyman.)

And some people live in apartments, like the Park Lane, whose very San Francisco doorman is pictured here. (Photo: Ione Hyman.)

79

Typical of an age and an era is this house at Broadway and Webster Streets. (Photo: Bob Hollingsworth.)

80

(Photo: Ione Hyman.)

(Photo: Bob Hollingsworth.)

The architectural details found on many of the houses and apartments are fascinating in themselves.

A corner of Whitney Warren's attractive apartment on the western side of
Telegraph Hill—the scene of many elegant soirées. (Photo: Jerome Zerbe.)

The Spreckels mansion, on Washington and Octavia, cost around $225,000 when it was built in 1911 and couldn't be duplicated for five times that today. (Photo: Bob Hollingsworth.)

The city is noted for its white, un-besooted buildings. Here an old house gets a new coat of paint. (Photo: Kurt Bank.)

Modern house on Vallejo Street, de-signed by Joseph Esherick. (Photo: Halberstadt.)

A doubly attractive invitation to rent a room. (Photo: Bob Hollingsworth.)

A row of typically San Francisco-style
houses. (Photo: Bob Hollingsworth.)

THE HILLS

For years people have persisted in voicing the myth that San Francisco, like Rome and Lisbon, is built on seven hills. Actually there are closer to forty.

Julia Altrocchi writes: "In the social topography of San Francisco the gilded migration has been from early fashionable Stockton Street to the Mission District to Rincon Hill and South Park to the south slope of Russian Hill to Nob Hill to Seacliff and Pacific Heights—a climb almost steadily upwards socially and topographically."

Russian Hill was eased into its name by the fact that some Russian sailors who died of scurvy were buried there. Natives enjoy scaring tourists by driving them down Filbert Street from Hyde to Leavenworth, a 37-per-cent grade.

The hills make it tough for dedicated skiers. (Photo: Miriam Young.)

On Telegraph Hill was a semaphore which in the gold-rush days would signal to the city that a ship was coming, and indicate its type and size so that the merchants and others could prepare for its arrival. So familiar were these signals that once when an actor burst into a living-room scene on the stage, flung his arms straight out, and bellowed out his line at the actress, "What does this mean?" the delighted audience called back: "Sidewheel steamer!"

Nob Hill, often called Nabob Hill because of bonanza kings and railroad pioneers who first built there, is still the fashionable center of town. Robert Louis Stevenson wrote of it, "Nor did I even neglect Nob Hill, which is itself a kind of slum, being the habitat of the mere millionaire." It boasts three fine hotels: the Huntington, the Fairmont (which tourists insist on calling the Fairmount), and the Mark Hopkins (locals call it the Mark; yokels call it the Hopkins).

Nob Hill has the University Club and the super-exclusive Pacific Union Club, the latter being housed in the old James Flood mansion, the only Nob Hill house not completely destroyed by the 1906 earthquake and fire.

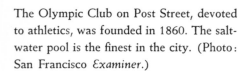

The mailman takes everything in his stride. (Photo: Peters.)

The Olympic Club on Post Street, devoted to athletics, was founded in 1860. The salt-water pool is the finest in the city. (Photo: San Francisco *Examiner*.)

Looking for a flat, everyone has two requirements—a view and a garden. But they seldom come together; one has to make a choice. (Photo: Jacqueline Paul.)

And, speaking of clubs, of which we have some interesting ones, just down the hill a ways on Taylor Street is the Bohemian Club. B. E. Lloyd, writing in *Lights and Shades*, called the Bohemian Club the most interesting of all.

It was organized April 1, 1872. Its membership numbers over two hundred and fifty persons. The badge or motto of this club is very suggestive. It consists of a shield upon which an "owl-eyed" owl, perched upon a grinning, brainless skull, stares ominously around; across his breast is traced the apt inscription, "Weaving spiders come not here." The inference might be drawn —it were better to have no brains at all, than to have webby brains.... Its members are necessarily journalists, authors, artists, actors, and musicians—professions requiring intellectual advancement. The entertainments given monthly (which the club terms "High Jinks"), are exceedingly interesting, and sometimes develop into real intellectual brilliancy.

Those "High Jinks" still go on and the annual sojourn at "the Grove" attracts renowned members from all over the United States.

The Olympic Club on Post Street, devoted to athletics, was founded in 1860.

A very stimulating club on the same street is the Press and Union League, which weekly features outstanding speakers who, when they speak from behind Bufano's black-cat statue, have the complete security of an off-the-record audience.

THE CABLE CARS

A cable car of the 1880s stops at California and Central (now California Street and Presidio). (Courtesy California Historical Society.)

90

And a modern cable car stops in front of the Hotel St. Francis on Union Square. (Photo: Bob Hollingsworth.)

The cable car is the most instantly San Franciscan symbol we have. The elimination of them, a proposition which is constantly threatened, seems like the most egregious act of idiocy ever considered by an otherwise sane city. Since it is hard to calculate in dollars just how much revenue the cable cars attract in the tourist trade, self-styled practical men running the city periodically point out that the cable cars lose money annually and are a nuisance to keep up compared to those nice, simple, redolent buses.

If the cable cars were removed, the tourist trade would of course not suddenly stop, but the disquieting feeling that "Frisco isn't the place it used to be" would surely begin to disenchant visitors from the day of their arrival.

The charming mechanical anachronism first appeared in 1873, the brain-child of a cable manufacturer named Andrew Hallidie, who invented the car because he felt sorry for the horses which often slipped and broke their legs on the steep hills. No one else would drive the contraption on its first ride down Clay Street, so Hallidie himself became the conductor. He braked it to a safe stop at the bottom of the hill, turned it around on a turntable, and then snagged the running wire rope in the slot to go back up. By 1890 the cable car was here to stay, and there were eight major cable-car systems operating within the city limits.

And stay it had better, or thousands of outraged San Franciscans will march on the

(Photo: Gene Wright.)

City Hall, in all probability led by the valiant Mrs. Hans Klussman, a surgeon's wife, who in 1947 conducted the heroic fight to save the cars virtually single-handed.

The inventor of the unique cable car is immortalized in the Hallidie Building, which stands at Sutter near Montgomery, where a bronze plaque proclaims: "Builder, Citizen, Regent—A Man of Integrity."

Lucius Beebe adds a postscript to this: "To San Franciscans, their town is not only a way of life; it is a religion. The cable cars are a tenet of it."

Rudyard Kipling, upon the occasion of his visit to the city in 1889, was awed by our mobile "tenet," and said, "I gave up asking questions about their mechanism . . . if it pleases Providence to make a car run up and down a slit in the ground for many miles, and if for two-pence-hapenny I can ride in that car, why should I seek reasons for that miracle?"

A fact many people don't know is that eight other American cities by 1887 had adopted cable cars: Chicago; Brooklyn; Kansas City, Missouri; St. Louis; Los Angeles; Oakland; Omaha; and Hoboken. All their cable cars have long since disappeared.

Probably the most durable of the cable-car anecdotes is the one Lucius Beebe quotes in *Cable Car Carnival:* "Early in the days of the cable when wind-up toys for children were still a novelty in the Christmas markets, a Chinese houseboy named Ching Pon was on his early morning way to work when he perceived a tram on the Hyde Street cable had become stalled because of some minor mechanical breakdown. Approaching the gripman in the hope of being of assistance he enquired gravely: 'Whattsa maller—stling bloke?' The phrase became a San Francisco wisecrack on all occasions for a decade or two!"

(Photo: Bob Hollingsworth.)

(Photo: Ruth Bernhard.)

The men who operate the cable cars seem to be a unique breed, often colorful and amusing, and always good anecdotal material. Witness this typical item from a recent column by Herb Caen:

Swung gracelessly aboard Powell cable and stood on back platform, where small tourist boy watching egg-eyed as conductor cranked hand brake. "What's that for?" kid finally asked. "Well, sonny," ans'd conductor pleasantly, "an old Chinaman lives down there in the slot, and he's so old he can't get up and down the hills without us. There's a dingbat on the end of this crank, see, and we hook onto his pigtail to help him along." Kid's eyes positively bursting as car started down other side of Nob Hill. "Think we got him okay," said conductor. Then he released hand brake and smote his forehead. "Darn!" he exclaimed. "Lost him!" Kid looked woefully into cable slot, almost teary-eyed. One ride *he*'ll never forget.

95

Every book on San Francisco has to have a picture of a cable car being turned, so here is a cable car being turned, on Powell Street. (Photo: Jerome Zerbe.)

Opposite: Visitors often remark that riding up and down the hills of San Francisco in a cable car is like riding in a roller coaster, but habitués nonchalantly take the cable cars—and the hills—as a matter of course. (Photo: Ruth Bernhard.)

THE BRIDGES

Three times as long as the Brooklyn Bridge, the Golden Gate Bridge is the longest single-span bridge in the world (4200 feet). Completed in 1937, at a cost of $35,000,000, it takes some 100,000 people a day across the entrance to San Francisco Bay.

It took 60,000 gallons of paint to paint the bridge when first built, and twenty-five painters are constantly applying the "international orange" color (which helps account for the $2200-per-day upkeep cost).

The Bay Bridge to Oakland and the East Bay cuts through Yerba Buena Island, (formerly and inelegantly Goat Island). It has an overall length of 8¼ miles (12 miles including approaches), of which 4½ miles are over water. Towering 474 to 519 feet above the water, it required 207,000 tons of steel and 118,000 gallons of paint, and many workmen's lives were lost. It was completed in 1936.

A depressing fact about the Golden Gate Bridge is its allure to would-be suicides; almost two hundred have gone over its rails in its twenty-two-year history, three of whom were friends of mine.

As for the name, Captain John Charles Frémont named "the Straits" the Golden Gate around 1850, writing: "To this Gate I gave the name 'Crysopylae' [sic] or Golden Gate, for the same reason that the Harbor of Byzantium was called 'Crysoceras' [sic] or Golden Horn."

The origin of the name San Francisco has already been touched on in this book, but the name of our state has never really been explained satisfactorily anywhere. In the *Annals of San Francisco,* published in 1854, the authors come up with as good an explanation as any:

> The etymology of the name CALIFORNIA is uncertain. Some writers have pretended that it is derived from the two Latin words *calida fornax,* or, in the Spanish language, *caliente fornalla* —a hot furnace. This, however, is doubted by Michael Venegas, a Mexican Jesuit, in his *Natural and Civil History of California* (2 vols., Madrid, 1758), a work of much research and high authority. In his opinion, the early Spanish discoverers did not name their new-found lands in this pedantic fashion. "I am therefore inclined to think," he says, "that this name owed its origin to some accident; possibly to some words spoken by the Indians, and misunderstood by the Spaniards," as happened in several other cases.
>
> The name *California* is first found in Bernal Diaz del Castillo, an officer who served under Hernando Cortez, in the conquest of Mexico, and who published a history of that extraordinary expedition; and is by him limited to a single bay on the coast.

Golden Gate Bridge, looking across at Marin County. This is
the world's longest single-span bridge. (Photo: Don Worth.)

This unusual picture of the Golden Gate Bridge was selected for the "Photography in the Fine Arts" exhibition at the Metropolitan Museum of Art in New York and added to the museum's permanent collection. (Photo: Emil Schulthess.)

Painting cables on the Golden Gate Bridge. (Photo: Mason Weymouth.)

(Photo:
Mason Weymouth.)

Here and on the opposite page are two views of the San Francisco-Oakland Bay Bridge. Next door to Berkeley and the great University of California, Oakland is kept busy with its steel, timber, canning, and shipping industries. It has large residential areas and is the seat of the venerable Mills College for Women.

(Photo: Jerome Zerbe.)

THE SHIPS AND THE BOATS

San Francisco is the gateway to the Orient, to Australia, to the fabled South Pacific, and, as Richard Henry Dana said, "the sole emporium of a new world, the Pacific." It has 18 miles of berthing space on the Embarcadero, and enough room all around the bay's 465 square miles to berth every craft afloat in the world at one time. It is the largest natural harbor in the world.

The famous home-owned Matson and American President steamship lines send thousands of tourists every month to Honolulu, Tahiti, and Japan.

There are twenty-five yacht harbors in the bay and about thirty classes of boats. The biggest race of the year is the Hearst Regatta in the spring. The funniest is the Annual Bullship Race, started by lawyer Charles O'Gara in 1953; contestants are required only to have a tiny El Toro sailing dinghy and a major lunacy, since the course is all the way from Sausalito, across the dangerous tides of the Golden Gate, to the St. Francis Yacht Harbor in San Francisco. One year a third of the entries capsized, but still over a hundred psychopaths turn out every "Sábado de Gloria" (Holy Saturday) to vie for the worthless El Matador Perpetual Trophy. Wives and friends prepare Irish coffee and wait tremulously on the greensward for the contestants to sail or be hauled into port.

Opposite: Moored at Pier 43 is the 256-foot square-rigged sailing vessel *Balclutha*, which was built in Scotland in 1886 and made seventeen trips around the Horn. It was engaged in the salmon trade in Alaska, has been used as a movie set, and is now preserved by the San Francisco Maritime Museum. (Photo: Tom King.)

104

Sunrise on San Francisco Bay—and a tug nudges a
freighter into the Embarcadero. (Photo: Jerry Stoll.)

Opposite: The Matson ship *Lurline* docks after a 4½-day trip from Hawaii.
Matson ships carry passengers to Australia and other South Pacific destinations.
(Photo: Tom King.)

Leading the field in the zany annual Bull-ship race is this eight-foot toro-class boat. (Photo: Barney Petersen.)

Heeling over in a race across the Gate. (Photo: San Francisco *Chronicle*.)

The great spring event for yachtsmen is the Hearst
Regatta. (Photo: San Francisco *Examiner*.)

Small boats and big boats—the harbor is full of them.   (Photo: Wes Pease.)

Over 170 steamship lines converge in San Francisco. Chief imports include raw silk, coffee, tea, sugar, coconut oil, and newsprint. Among the principal exports are canned fruits, barley, lumber, oil and gasoline, machinery, cotton, canned salmon, metals, and automobiles.

111

Looking beyond the stern of the *Balclutha,* one sees the island of Alcatraz smoldering in the bay. It was named "Alcatraces" in 1775 after the many pelicans on its twelve-acre area; the birds disappeared in the mid-nineteenth century. "The Rock" became a federal penitentiary in 1934. The total capacity for inmates is 364, and it takes almost that many guards and employees to keep them there. Not long ago John Updike published this sardonic little poem in *The New Yorker,* entitled "Scenic":

O when in San Francisco do
As natives do: they sit and stare
And smile and stare again. The view
Is visible from anywhere.

Here hills are white with houses whence,
Across a multitude of sills,
The owners, lucky residents,
See other houses, other hills.

The meanest San Franciscan knows,
No matter what his past has been,
There are a thousand patios
Whose view he is included in.

The Golden Gate, the cable cars,
Twin Peaks, the Spreckels habitat,
The local ocean, sun, and stars—
When fog falls, one admires *that.*

Here homes are stacked in such a way
That every picture window has
An unmarred prospect of the Bay
And, in its center, Alcatraz.

(Photo: Conrad.)

Cooking the crabs. (Photo: Jacqueline Paul.)

FISHERMAN'S WHARF

In 1900 the state decided that the area near the foot of Taylor and Leavenworth Streets would be given over to the fishermen and their boats. Among the famous old fisher families were Castagnola, Geraldi, Sabella, DiMaggio, and Alioto, all of whom own successful restaurants there today.

The most common fish in the bay are the surf perch, herring, rock cod, sole, salmon, and striped bass, but most purchasers go to the wharf for the delicious crab, clams, Olympia oysters, abalone, sand dabs, and tiny bay shrimp.

There are more than 2000 men and 350 vessels engaged in the fishing industry here, and their annual catch is 300,000,000 pounds per year. Sardines account for most of that, with crabs sidling in second.

Here Mrs. Edwin Callan looks over a selection of crabs for dinner. (Photo: Jerome Zerbe.)

An old-time Italian fisherman baiting hooks in preparation for deep-sea fishing. Most commercial fishing boats in the harbor are run by Italians.

Tarantino's is one of the
several famous restaurants
on Fisherman's Wharf.
(Photo: Mason Weymouth.)

Salmon fisherman. (Photo: Jacqueline Paul.)

The seas of San Francisco give—and they can take away, as this highly dramatic photograph demonstrates. After a morning of crab fishing, Domenico Tringali was on his way back to Fisherman's Wharf on his boat *Baby* when a steering cable parted off Point Lobos. He managed to leap ashore just before the boat crashed on the rocks. Tringali was not injured but he could not bear to watch his uninsured livelihood being pounded to bits by the waves and he turned his face away in anguish just as alert photographer Ray Morris arrived on the scene. (Courtesy San Francisco *Examiner*.)

Maiden Lane. (Photo: Tom King.)

UNION SQUARE

Presented to the city in 1850 by Mayor John White Geary, Union Square is presumed to have earned its name from the mass meetings by Northerners on the eve of the Civil War.

Above is a shot of Maiden Lane.

This now highly respectable little thoroughfare, which gives onto Union Square and extends only two blocks, was once known as Morton Street, or "Iodoform Alley." Habitat of the infamous Iodoform Kate and others of her ilk, it has had as lurid a little history as any part of the city. Oscar Lewis writes of it in *Bay Window Bohemia*:

Here was an assemblage of resorts as varied—and depraved—as any in the city. Not only did it shelter harlots of all nations—including French, Chinese, Negroes, Mexicans, and Americans —but it was the hangout, too, of pickpockets, dope peddlers, and thugs of every description.

Although Morton Street, as stated, cut across the very center of the retail shopping district, it was scrupulously avoided by the town's respectable women, for to set foot within its con-

Opposite: Union Square with the Hotel St. Francis in the background.
(Photo: Bob Hollingsworth.)

120

fines was considered a serious breach of decorum. To guard against that possibility there was usually a policeman stationed at each end of the street charged with warning away the curious.

When, shortly after the turn of the century, the wily Abe Reuf made himself political boss of the town, he ordered a clean-up campaign during which every Morton Street resort was closed and padlocked. Moreover, unlike most such campaigns—which usually lasted only a week or two —this one remained in force for month after month. Meantime the property owners, one by one, got discouraged and sold out, the buyer in each case being an agent for the same Reuf. Then having picked up nearly all the houses at bargain prices, he lifted the embargo and the street was presently again going full blast. It continued to boom until the entire area was laid waste by the fire of 1906. Today the former Morton Street is a thoroughfare given over to gift shops, tearooms, cocktail bars, and the like, all of unimpeachable respectability.

Chic shoppers usually take time for luncheon at the El Prado, or catch a fashion show, as here at the Hotel St. Francis.

(Photo: San Francisco *Chronicle*.)

122

Blum's, a San Francisco institution, has several branches around town, and here, at the one next to I. Magnin's on Union Square, I snapped Suzanne Barton, a typical (happily) San Francisco girl having her lunch.

Gump's, a favorite store for ninety-three years, is only half a block off Union Square on Post Street. It's not only good luck to give the Buddha a coin; it helps charity as well. The store's jade collection alone is known the world over. The owner, Richard Gump, plays wonderfully atrocious music in an amateur German oom-pah band. (Cartoonist George Lichty is another culprit in the organization.) (Photo: Conrad.)

Once upon a time Union Square was nothing more than part of a huge sand bank
known as O'Farrell Mountain. Now, bounded by hotel- and store-lined Powell, Geary,

Post, and Stockton Streets, the square represents the heart of the city's fashionable shopping center. It is equally popular with the pigeons. (Photo: Gene Wright.)

Among Union Square's many elegant shops is Laykin's jewelry emporium, which is the town's favorite along with Shreve's. Boss A.A. "Bud" Ehresmann shows off a valuable bracelet. (Photo: Conrad.)

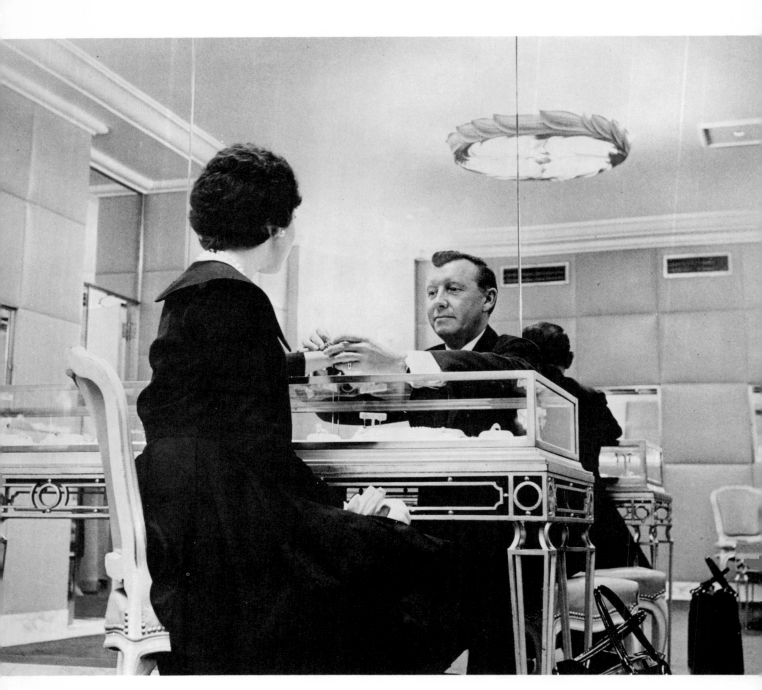

(Photo: Tom King.)

San Francisco is a city of flowers. Visitors are always impressed by the quantity of flower stands, and by such outstanding shops as Podesta and Baldocchi on Grant Avenue. Here a girl stops at a flower stand in the shape of a cable car near Paul Verdier's venerable (1850) City of Paris department store.

Will Irwin, in his 1906 tribute to the city, wrote of the young San Franciscan woman: "The mixed stock has given her that regularity of features which goes with a blend of bloods; the climate has perfected and rounded her figure, out-of-door exercise from earliest youth has given her a deep bosom; the cosmetic mists have made her complexion soft and brilliant."

Next page: The column in the center of Union Square commemorates the victory of Admiral Dewey at Manila Bay in 1898. The sculptor, Robert Aitken, is said to have used Alma Spreckels as his model for the bronze statue at the top. (Photo: Bob Hollingsworth.)

(Photo: Gene Wright.)

TELEGRAPH HILL

The night photo of Coit Tower was taken from Castle Street. The tower, which crowns the hill where once the semaphore station stood, was designed by Arthur Brown, Jr., with funds left for it by Lillie Hitchcock Coit upon her death in 1929. It is a monument to San Francisco's firemen; the city, understandably, has always been keenly fire-conscious and the department is considered the finest in America. The donor, who in 1863 was made an honorary member of Knickerbocker Engine Company No. 5, signed herself

Opposite: A prize-winning photo shows a night-time view of Coit Tower through Castle Street. (Photo: Royal Bradbury.)

"Lillie Hitchcock Coit—5" until the day she died. A madcap in her early years (see page 17), she was forced into exile from her beloved San Francisco by a tragedy. Oscar Lewis writes of it thus in *Bay Window Bohemia:*

> As time passed, the indomitable Lillie came to occupy a less conspicuous place in the public eye, her earlier escapades forgotten by all but a few old-timers. Soon after the turn of the century, however, she was again projected into the limelight, this time through no choice of her own. In the summer of 1904, while staying at the Palace Hotel, she was one evening entertaining an old friend, a Major McClung, in her suite when a distant relative—whom she had hired to look after her San Francisco properties—entered and, locking the door behind him, drew a revolver and leveled it at her.
>
> Before the intruder could fire, McClung sprang on him, and in the struggle that followed the weapon was discharged, the ball striking the major, who fell to the floor. The crazed man —no reason for his behavior was ever learned—then turned on the lady herself. She, however, far from being cowed, faced his gun unflinchingly, meanwhile reasoning with him, and to such good effect that in the end he pocketed his weapon and hurried downstairs to summon the house physician. Major McClung died the next day and his assailant, having been pronounced insane, was committed to an asylum.
>
> The affair, of course, created a sensation, and to escape the publicity that followed, Mrs. Coit fled to Paris. While there she learned that the demented man had vowed to kill her should he ever regain his freedom; the result was that not until the other's death some twenty years later did she return to San Francisco. She was close to eighty when she finally came back, and so ill that much of the next five years were spent on a hospital bed, where she died in the summer of 1929. Today Coit Tower on Telegraph Hill, together with a statute honoring the volunteer fire fighters of the early town, in nearby Washington Square, stands as a memorial to this most colorful of San Francisco's daughters.

Many writers and artists still live on Telegraph Hill, called "San Francisco's Greenwich Village." Traditionally they patronize "Speedy's" all-purpose store, and attend the annual street fair. But it has become increasingly fashionable and too high-priced for many of their incomes. Tourists and natives alike enjoy the three restaurants, Julius' Castle, the Shadows, and the Old Spaghetti Factory.

Back in the 1890s *the* Telegraph Hill restaurant for the literati was Luna's. It was tucked away at the bottom of the hill at Vallejo Street and Grant Avenue (then Dupont Street), and apparently when a restaurant was tucked in those days it really stayed tucked. San Franciscans always have liked hard-to-find night spots, but this was unrivaled, according to Frank Norris:

> Luna's Mexican restaurant has no address. It is on no particular street, at no particular corner, even its habitués, its most enthusiastic devotees, are unable to locate it upon demand. . . . It is "over there in the quarter," "not far from the cathedral there." One could find it if one started out with that intent; but to direct another there—no, that is out of the question. It *can* be reached by following the alleys of Chinatown. You will come out of the last alley —the one where the slave girls are—upon the edge of the Mexican quarter, and by going ahead for a block or two, and by keeping a sharp lookout to the right and left you will hit upon it. It is always to be searched for. Always to be discovered."

The Co-Existence Bagel Shop on upper Grant Avenue. (Photo: Gene Wright.)

NORTH BEACH

North Beach was the dream of Harry Meiggs, who bought up acres of land there around 1854, expecting the city to expand in that direction and make it the center of town. Unfortunately, progress went the other way. Heavily in debt, Meiggs sneaked out of town bound for Tahiti, leaving dozens of people swindled. (He turned up in Peru later, where he became a railroad pioneer, and died a respected millionaire.)

North Beach is made up of many nationalities, but the 60,000 Italians are what flavor the place and good Italian restaurants abound—Amelio's, Fior d'Italia, Vannessi's, and New Joe's, to name a few. Pizzerias such as Lupo's and the Sorrento fling their products skyward with éclat and abandon, and their crusts rival Naples' finest.

Upper Grant Avenue is the playground of Bohemia. The Co-Existence Bagel Shop is the nucleus of Beatnikland, the hangout of the self-styled intellectual nihilistic group whose members think that all their generation is "beat." Because beards are their badge, many real artists and writers who have worn beards for years are shaving them off so as not to be confused with the "Beatniks," as Herb Caen dubbed them so permanently.

133

After visitors to the city have exclaimed about the views and the hills, the next thing usually mentioned is the wonderful "French" bread. The picture on this page shows an Italian sour-dough factory in action. (The next thing inevitably mentioned about the city is the politeness of cab drivers and the fact that they always get out to open the door for their passengers.)

Inside a typical Italian store and delicatessen. (Photo: Jacqueline Paul.)

At Sorrento's, pizza flinging is a fine art. (Photo: Sandino.)

Opposite: Old-world recipes are still used in most
North Beach homes. (Photo: Ginny Leonard.)

137

A game of cards

. . . and a game of bocce ball.

Opposite: In the same North Beach *boîte,* the Bocce Ball, old-time opera singer Meloni sits humming a Puccini aria to himself.

(Photos: Jacqueline Paul.)

THE WATER

It's cold. And sometimes sharks attack swimmers brave enough to defy the temperature and the undertow. But it's wet and usually clean, and it looks blue and inviting from the Golden Gate Bridge and the waves are high and white at China Beach, and the seals on the rocks near the Cliff House love it, and so do the abalone and the Bay shrimp and the pismo clams, and so do the old men at Aquatic Park who take off their shoes and let its coolness make their toes young.

(Photo: Jacqueline Paul.)

141   (Photo: Robert L. Fraser.)

THE BEACHES

"How *white* your city is!" people exclaim when they first see it, and one is reminded that San Francisco *is* cleaner-looking than most big cities. In the same way the beaches seem more scrubbed than others, as though Lewis Carroll's seven maids with their seven mops had been working overtime. San Franciscans, when they tire of the city's beaches, like to drive to Bolinas or Stinson Beach in the north or to Aptos and Pebble Beach in the south.

(Photo: Robert S. Riley.)

Ocean Beach.

(Photo: Robert L. Fraser.)

CHINATOWN

The shoemaker.

Children of High Class.

Arnold Genthe snapped these three photos in old Chinatown. Except for a few photos, Genthe's hundreds of studies of the city went up in flames when the earthquake struck. He used to carry a very small camera and hide it under his coat because of the Chinese fear of "the devil box." (Photos courtesy California Historical Society.)

Pipe Dream.

The first Chinese settlers, two men and a woman, were believed to have come from Hong Kong in 1848 as servants of the Charles Gillespies. Although about 4000 Chinese came to California in 1851 there were only seven women among them; it was said that owing to this shortage a certain Madame Ah Toy was paid gold dust as the price for simply gazing on her beautiful face.

Many Chinese came to make their fortunes in gold and then returned with it to China. Prejudice against the "heathen Chinee" reached a high peak during the 1870s and 1880s, when Charles Crocker hired about 10,000 Chinese to work on the railroads for cheaper wages than those of the Irish. Dennis Kearney labeled them "Crocker's pets" and howled, "The Chinese must go!" He organized a group of rabble-rousers into the Workingman's Party and went so far as to attack Mr. Crocker's mansion. In 1882 an act was passed by Congress limiting the admission of Chinese laborers.

In order to protect the Chinese from hoodlums and act as a type of tribunal in settling disputes among the Chinese, the organization of Six Companies was founded in 1876. Other organizations were the Four Families and the tongs—the trade guilds.

145

Till the 1900s Chinatown suffered many tong wars and was terrorized by rough characters such as "Little Pete" and his tong, the Gi Sin Seer. ("Little Pete" got off guard once, relaxed for a moment in a barber's chair, and was shot to death.)

During the earthquake dozens of people were killed in Chinatown, for many of the dwellings there were underground.

After the fire, Chinatown rebuilt itself, and the era of crime was ended; today it is the major tourist attraction of San Francisco, as well as a home for 25,000 Chinese. More than that, it is an integral part of every San Franciscan's life. As the venerable periodical, *The Argonaut*, said in a recent editorial:

Something we can scarcely imagine is San Francisco without the Chinese. They came here with the earliest settlers, in the Manila galleons that touched at northern Oriental ports and the Gold Rush, which gave such immense impetus to maritime traffic, brought them here in great numbers. Humble as were their functions in this first boisterous, burgeoning society, the Chinese character, the Chinese mind, and their ancient, inbred culture made an immediate and lasting impression on the first city of the Western frontier.

Can it be that there is something essentially Oriental in the landscape, in the delicate and definitive lines of sudden hills, the flora, sturdily decorative rather than lush, the enamel-like colors of hills, sea and sky? It is all concentrated here, around de Portolás "waste of water"; as what we know as Chinatown is set within metropolitan San Francisco. No Great Wall gives

146

it sweep and broad-based boundary, nor is there room for a Forbidden City, with its inspired used of space wherein to mount courts and pagodas; but Chinatown has its own pagodas, with multiple curvilinear eaves, its gilt and scarlet lacquer, and its ghostly pavilions of the mind and spirit, to shelter the genii of the Oriental community.

To the Chinese we owe much, not only what is immediately satisfying to the eye, but also that which is so arresting as to instruct taste and tease the intellect. Their old, old men, whose tongue we cannot easily learn, speak to us with their seamed dark-ivory faces; in their enchanting children, plump mandarins in miniature, we see reborn the graces of a civilization that was old before ours began.

Behind these familiar scenes we sense a philosophy to which we can profitably aspire; as beyond the pungent odors of fish and duck and spice we catch the subtle fragrances of incense and tea; and above the cacophony of the narrow streets we hear the mellow tongues of golden temple bells.

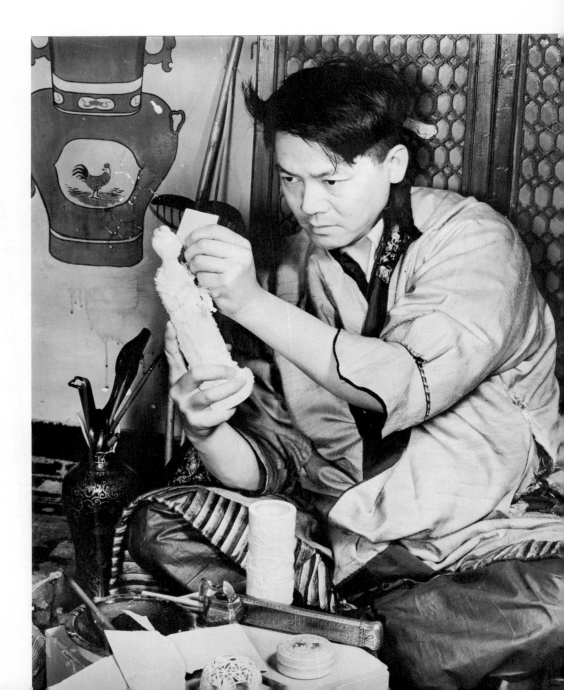

An ivory worker in one of Grant Avenue's many fascinating shops. Some shop windows feature the weird pharmacopoeia of Oriental healing, such as tiger bones, powdered antlers, and dried lizards and frogs. (Photo: Moulin Studios.)

San Franciscans like to boast that Chinatown is the largest Chinese colony outside of China, and, except for Singapore, it is. Furthermore, it supports as many as three newspapers and only one has an English page. Although nearly all the inhabitants speak English, many old-world customs and costumes still prevail.

(Photos: Charles Wong.)

Tourists are fascinated by the exotic shops and strange foods and smells along Grant Avenue. (Photo: Jacqueline Paul.)

A citizen of China's annex in America shadow-boxes in Chinese New Year festival. (Photo: Jacqueline Paul.)

(Photo: Jacqueline Paul.)

Chinese New Year "Lion Dance." Fireworks are also part of the
show; only here are they legal in fire-leery San Francisco, as they
are considered part of a religious ceremony.

153

(Photo: J. E. Cakebread.)

Chinese New Year custom of collecting money. (Photo: Jacqueline Paul.)

A happy family party at Gon Sam Mue's, whose brother Johnny Kan owns the city's most successful Chinese restaurant. Chinese food is so popular that San Francisco has about twice as many Chinese restaurants outside Chinatown as in it. (Photo: Mason Weymouth.)

155

A visiting Oriental diplomat who called at the wrong apartment and had some laundry thrust at him by an American housewife is said to have remarked politely, "Madame, all laundries may be Chinese, but not all Chinese are laundrymen." There do, however, seem to be a great many Chinese laundries, both in and out of Chinatown. (Photo: Paul Hassel.)

Washington and Grant. (Photo: Conrad.)

This solid San Franciscan could very well be a citizen of old Hong Kong.

Opposite: A Chinese child sails through the air at the children's playground. (Photo: Conrad.)

The famous Victorian Conservatory. (Photo: Jerome Zerbe.)

GOLDEN GATE PARK

Nine city blocks wide and four and a half miles long, "the Park" is a joy to the city and a living monument to its creators.

When the city acquired the then barren land in 1869 for $1,000,000, many people thought it was crazy. For eighteen years the newspapers poked fun at the "bad bargain." One said, "Of all the elephants . . . San Franciscans ever owned they now have the largest and heaviest in the shape of 'Golden Gate Park.'"

In 1887, when Uncle John McLaren became park superintendent, he planted the sand dunes with lupine and sand grass and fertilized them with street sweepings. For fifty-six years he devoted himself to beautifying the area, his term as superintendent ending only with his death in 1943 at the age of ninety-seven. Today the park has five thousand kinds of plants, a conservatory, open-air concert area, a lovely Japanese tea garden, the fine M. H. De Young Museum, the California Academy of Sciences, the renowned Steinhart aquarium, and a children's playground, complete with carousel.

Japanese Tea Garden. (Photo: Gene Wright.)

Baby airing is one of the many ways citizens really use their park. (Photo: Ruth Bernhard.)

Stow Lake. (Photo: Jacqueline Paul.)

An old-time custom, the band concert in
the park. (Photo: Mason Weymouth.)

Mrs. Mason Weymouth, well-known musician, enjoys the
carousel with her daughter. (Photo: Mason Weymouth.)

Right: The M. H. De Young Memorial Museum of fine art is San Francisco's largest museum. The collection contains master paintings and is particularly strong in Aztec, Incan, Mayan, and pre-Columbian American art. (Photo: J. E. Cakebread.)

Bibliophiles also love the park. (Photo: Pearson.)

The city's newspaper photographers traditionally dress in tails for opera opening night and are often more sartorially correct than their subjects. On hand here are Duke Downey, Ken McLaughlin, and Bob Campbell. (Photo: San Francisco *Chronicle*.)

THE OPERA

The Opera Association was begun in 1923 by Gaetano Merola, and its Opera House was the first municipal one in the nation. The city emerges in all its elegance for its season every fall, and to admit to not liking the art form is positively un-San Franciscan. Back in 1913 Leoncavallo himself conducted *I Pagliacci* at the old Tivoli.

The diamond horseshoe.

Entr'acte.

After the opera season there follows a gaudy hoedown known as the Fol-de-Rol, where all the singers perform, people dance, and balloons cascade from the ceiling. (Photo: Kurt Bank.)

Chico at the opera. (Photo: Art Frisch.)

Heiress Dorothy Fritz, accompanied by Philip Stevenson, poses for photographers before going up to a box on opening night. They'll be two of the 3285 people the Opera House holds. (Photo: Bill Young.)

Herb Caen — Mr. San Francisco — whose daily column starts the day off for hundreds of thousands of San Franciscans, dances (center of the floor) at the opera's Fol-de-Rol. Relaxing at the table immediately below him is Thomas Carr Howe (with glasses), director of the California Palace of the Legion of Honor. (Photo: N. R. Farbman.)

Here, dining at Jack's, are financier Louis Lurie, producer Randolph Hale, and Edward Everett Horton and his mother.

(Photo: San Francisco *Examiner*.)

NIGHT LIFE

Los Angeles people frequently speak of "going to the city"—meaning San Francisco, not their own metropolis. The reason they give is often "to have some fun and get some good food."

San Francisco has a reputation for fine food, though I'm not sure it is always earned. Los Angeles itself has three fine restaurants that are as good as or better than the best of San Francisco. We have a great deal of good Italian cooking, but few of our French restaurants are up to New York's, for example.

The Palace Hotel—and I wonder if San Franciscans will ever deign to add the recently acquired and resented "Sheraton" appendage—is one of the more valid reasons for San Francisco's culinary fame. Shown opposite is Lucien, one of the hotel's famous past chefs for the elegant Garden Court Dining Room.

San Francisco likes restaurants with a no-frills-or-nonsense *décor* about them, such as the Original Cold Day Restaurant, which, like the Poodle Dog, dates back to Gold Rush days. It is said that the Poodle Dog, formerly on Clay and Dupont (Grant Avenue now), was originally named the *Poulet d'Or*, but the first Pony Express rider couldn't pronounce it. This story, however, like the establishment's excellent food, should be taken *cum grano salis*.

Trader Vic's (either local or Oakland) is one of the finest restaurants, and certainly the San Francisco version is the Social Register's favorite rendezvous. Victor Bergeron, "Trade" himself, started the place twenty-five years ago in Oakland as Hinky Dink's.

Other fine restaurants are Ernie's, with its expensive-bordello *décor*; the Blue Fox, the movie stars' favorite; Alexis' Tangier on Nob Hill for kebab; India House for curry and Hindu waiters; Yamato, for atmospheric sukiyaki; Johnny Kan's for excellent Chinese

166

food; the Fleur de Lys for French food by candlelight. After the theater, it's Enrico's Coffee House, the Papagayo Room, Shanghai Lil's, or the Lochinvar Room at the Mark.

And among the more modest places are Monroe's, Adolph's, the New Pisa, and the Copper Lantern.

While there are some 1330 bars (as compared to 438 churches!), night-clubbing in the strict sense of the word is sometimes disappointing to visitors who come expecting the spirit of the Barbary Coast. The closest thing to a lavish spa is the Venetian Room at the Fairmont, or perhaps Bimbo's 365 Club. San Franciscans seem to prefer the less elegant *boîtes*, such as the "hungry i," Bee and Ray Goman's "Gay Nineties," the Sinaloa, the Bocce Ball, the Purple Onion, or La Bodega.

Left: Mrs. Thomas Carr Howe, Lily Pons, and Mrs. Robert Watt Miller dining at the Hotel St. Francis.

Below: Lucien, famous former chef of the Palace Hotel. (Photo: Mason Weymouth.)

Relaxing in style at Alexis' Tangier is syndicated and avidly read Stanton Delaplane, the city's roving-est reporter.

(Photo: Romaine Skelton.)

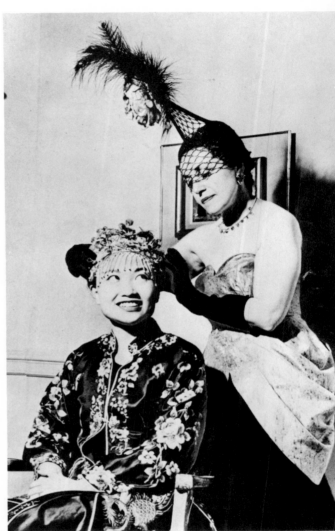

Below: Ceramist and author Jade Snow Wong and Mrs. George Mardikian, wife of the restaurateur and author are off to a fancy dress ball. (Photo: Barney Petersen.)

Mrs. Ambrose Diehl, director of the State Department's Reception Center in San Francisco, welcomes the many foreign notables who arrive in the city. Here she greets Princess Soraya, the former wife of the Shah of Iran. (Photo: Diehl.)

For years the E. Pym Joneses have made every opening night of every major function in the city, and it's rumored that a theater curtain just wouldn't go up if they weren't in their orchestra seats. (Photo: Harold Mack.)

Film people (such as Alfred Hitchcock and Kim Novak, shown in the photo above) seem to gravitate toward Ernie's plush restaurant with its turn-of-the-century *décor*.

Dmitri "Poom" de Ralguine, ex-tutor to the Czar's family, Russian scholar, and *bon vivant*, dances with La Vicomtesse de Bonchamps at the annual debutante cotillion. (Photo: Barney Petersen.)

Al Williams' Papagayo Room is probably the town's favorite after-theater eating place. With him here is one of his *papagayos*, a hyacinthine macaw yclept Macgregor and worth $1200.

(Photo: Romain.)

Henri Lenoir, *bohème extraordinaire*, collects paintings, old postcards, and odd types in his Vesuvio, a colorful North Beach watering hole. The figure over the bar *could* be a customer, but it happens to be a dummy, a portrait of the proprietor. (Photo: Stearns.)

Opposite: For *some* reason El Matador is my favorite after-theater spot, and I find my steps leading me back to it time and time again. (Photo: *Life*.)

And here is Victor Bergeron, proprietor of Trader Vic's.

Jazzman Turk Murphy plays his wonderful "San Francisco style" in a *boîte* in North Beach. (Photo: Gordon Peters.)

Crackling vibe maestro Cal Tjader can usually be found at the Blackhawk, a jazz buffs' mecca.

Below: At Ann's 440 Mr. Walter Hart, billed as "the male Sophie Tucker," bumps and grinds his way through an act.

(Photo: Carolyn Jones.)

And one of the town's favorite entertainers, the flamboyant Inez Torres, does the same. (Photo: Carolyn Jones.)

The Kingston Trio serve it up at the "hungry i." (Photo: Banducci.)

Floor show at Bee and Ray Goman's "Gay Nineties."

Jack Falvey's zoo includes the Van Ness beer emporium (*below*) called the Monkey Inn, a coffee house called the Crocodile Casbah, the hamburger hippodrome the Hippo, and a liquor store down the street called the Giraffe. The Monkey Inn is a sawdust-pianola place which appeals to the college set.

Above: For years "the girl in the fishbowl" has been a major attraction at Bimbo's. By a series of mirrors a naked girl (in a room downstairs) is made to look as though she were swimming around with the guppies.

Mary Tong looked the spirit of old China as I took this photograph in her atmospheric den, Shanghai Lil's, but she was born and brought up in San Francisco.

Beniamino Bufano, leading sculptor in San Francisco. (Photo: Jacqueline Paul.)

THE ARTS

San Francisco has prided itself on its contributions and contributors to the arts almost from the beginning of its history.

It's a highly musical city. For example, in 1911 San Francisco became the first to have a symphony assisted by public funds; it also was the first to admit women to the playing personnel.

Its great interest in the graphic arts and its roster of fine artists start back with the days of William Keith, the fine landscape painter, and of Arthur Putnam, the brilliant sculptor of animals. Today our three principal art museums are really used and enjoyed by the public and are active institutions constantly arranging for and planning new exhibitions. Two intelligent critics on the morning newspapers, Messrs. Alexander Fried and Alfred Frankenstein, aid and abet the high standard that prevails.

The city's literary heritage is well known, going back proudly to Mark Twain, Jack London, Robert Louis Stevenson, Frank Norris, Joaquin Miller, and Stewart Edward White. Bret Harte, Maxwell Anderson, and Sinclair Lewis were newspapermen here in the early days, and so was the vitriolic, brilliant Ambrose Bierce, who disappeared mysteriously from the face of the earth in Mexico when he was 71. (I shall always be grateful to Bierce for the "leads" of his many stories, particularly the one which begins, "Early one June morning in 1872 I murdered my father—an act which made a deep impression on me at the time.")

Another pioneer of belles-lettres in San Francisco was Gelett Burgess, of "Purple Cow" fame. In the mid-1890s he started a monthly magazine called *The Lark*, which was

176

Enrique Jorda rehearses a section of the San Francisco Symphony Orchestra. (Photo: Miriam Young.)

of high originality and great influence. It attracted many fine writers and among other things coined the words "blurb" and "bromide." Oscar Lewis, in *Bay Window Bohemia*, writes of it:

> By the end of its first year the little monthly had attained a circulation of 3000 copies, at which figure it stood as long as it continued to be published. In the beginning its price was five cents a copy or one dollar a year—Burgess, as he later confessed, had never been good at mathematics. At the end of the first twelve numbers, however, the single-copy price was raised to ten cents, with the yearly subscription remaining the same.
>
> Advertising was for the most part shunned, the only exceptions being occasional notices of books for sale at the shop of the publisher and, in No. 5, a full page was taken by Harrold, Belcker & Allen, the firm for which the editor was working as a designer. This stated concisely: "Old furniture made new. New furniture made old. Middle-aged furniture preserved. Black walnut furniture destroyed." Burgess was suspected of having written that copy; he almost certainly wrote a number of other pseudo ads that appeared from time to time, clever take-offs on the style and methods of the copy writers of the day. One was a grave announcement of a forthcoming book by architect Willis Polk, a massive tome entitled *Architecture Moderne*, the edition of which was to be limited to three copies, each handsomely bound in "half-chicken leather."

Then there were Gertrude Atherton, Peter B. Kyne, and Saroyan and Steinbeck. And, though I don't suppose we can call him a San Franciscan, Robert Frost *was* born here.

Two good critics, Luther Nichols and William Hogan, of the *Examiner* and the *Chronicle*, respectively, stimulate our literary clime.

Today our most active writers are C. S. Forester, Erskine Caldwell, Mark Harris, C. Y. Lee, Walter Van Tilburg Clark, Kenneth Patchen, Mark Schorer, Jessamyn West, Evan Connell, Ernest Gann, Niven Busch, Oakley Hall, Calvin Kentfield, and Robin White. And among our philosophers are Mortimer J. Adler and S. I. Hayakawa.

(Photo: Joe Rosenthal.)

At one of the many literary gatherings the author of this book and Lucius Beebe chat with Kathleen Norris, who, though over eighty, is one of the city's liveliest, most prolific, and best-loved writers. Beebe commutes from Virginia City, Nevada, where he publishes the antique, spry *Territorial Enterprise*. Fine historian and lucullan, Lucius shrugs at life and says simply, as he boards his private railroad car, valued at $128,000, "I admire to live well." This he does with a gusto and a flourish that San Franciscans of the turn of the century would have understood and applauded.

Poet Lawrence Ferlinghetti in his paperback book store, City Lights, in North Beach. (Photo: Jacqueline Paul.)

Novelist Erskine Caldwell is a relatively recent but fervent San Franciscan. People are surprised to find him very un-Caldwellish, urbane, sophisticated, affable, and totally unlike the people he writes about. (Photo: San Francisco *Chronicle*.)

As for the younger group of *fauves*, such as Lawrence Ferlinghetti, Allen Ginsberg, and Jack Kerouac—well, Henry Miller, who lives southward in the Robinson Jeffers country, wrote of them in "The San Francisco Scene":

Today it is not communities or groups who seek to lead "the good life" but isolated individuals. The majority of these, at least from my observation, are young men who have already had a taste of professional life, who have already been married and divorced, who have already served in the armed forces and seen a bit of the world.... Utterly disillusioned, this new breed of experimenter is resolutely turning his back on all that he once held true and viable, and is making a valiant effort to start anew. Starting anew, for this type, means leading a vagrant's life, tackling anything, clinging to nothing, reducing one's needs and one's desires, and eventually— out of a wisdom born of desperation—leading the life of an artist. Not, however, the type of artist we are familiar with. An artist, rather, whose sole interest is in creating, an artist who is indifferent to reward, fame, success. One, in short, who is reconciled from the outset to the fact that the better he is the less chance he has of being accepted at face value. These young men, usually in their late twenties or early thirties, are now roaming about in our midst like anonymous messengers from another planet.... When the smashup comes, as now seems inevitable, they will know how to get along without cars, without refrigerators, without vacuum cleaners, electric razors, and all the other "indispensables."

My own favorite comment on Kerouac, and on the group as a whole, was made by the *Manchester Guardian*, which said that Kerouac "too frequently sounds like a bad translation from the Czech."

179

(Photo: Gene Wright.)

Among our artists are Dong Kingman, Frank Ashley, Louis Macouillard, Antonio Sotomayor, Ralph DuCasse, Richard Diebenkorn, Luke Gibney, Robert Watson, Jean Varda. Dean of sculptors is Benny

180

Bufano, who once cut off a finger and sent it to President Wilson as a protest against war. Another of our noted sculptors in the classic tradition is Spero Anargyros, shown here in his North Beach Studio.

181

Dong Kingman instructs students in water-color painting
on Fisherman's Wharf. (Photo San Francisco *Examiner*.)

San Francisco has many art lovers, both young and old.
Permanent collections are on view at the M. H. De Young
Memorial Museum, the Palace of the Legion of Honor,
and the San Francisco Museum of Art. (Photo: Jacqueline
Paul.)

San Francisco State College has what must be the best-equipped theater, professional or otherwise, in the West. The college's theatrical presentations are consistently excellent; one of the best recently was *The Taming of the Shrew,* shown above. (Photo: Melliar.)

San Francisco has always been a dance-conscious town. The San Francisco Ballet is the only resident **company** based outside of New York. (Photo: Jacqueline Paul.)

A crowd at the Jazz Cellar on Green Street in North Beach, listening to poetry being read to jazz, a combination that flowered in San Francisco. (Photo: Jerry Stoll.)

A friendly Italian in the Valley of the Moon Creamery, North Beach, where it's not unusual to stand on a street corner and hear three different languages spoken in that many minutes. (Photo: Jacqueline Paul.)

THE PEOPLE

In 1910 the population of the city was 400,000, and since then it has risen approximately 100,000 each decade. What are those some 825,000 people like?

In 1875 the San Francisco *Newsletter* said, "The people of California and more especially the people of San Francisco have more exuberance than any other people since the Athenians of the days of Pericles." There seems to be little reason to amend that statement.

Here are photos of everyday San Franciscans of varying cultures going about their everyday jobs and pleasures with that quiet exuberance which seems to be indigenous to citizens of this city.

An out-of-town friend of mine said, as we passed Union Square the other day, "Look at the normal, relaxed expressions on the people as they go about their shopping and business—these aren't the harried and hurried and haunted types you see so often in most big cities of this country."

Yes, they seem happy. But all is not roses, of course. San Franciscans do appear to be a contented, adjusted breed. Yet what about the puzzling and alarming statistics? The rate of alcoholism is by far the highest in the nation, with the death rate from cirrhosis 3.5 times higher than the national level, more bars per square foot than any other city, and an average of 4.57 gallons of distilled spirits every year—several times the national level. Problem drinkers are estimated to number as high as one in every six adults, whereas the average of the rest of the nation is less than one in sixteen.

The narcotic problem is a serious one in spite of the vigilant Colonel George White of the Narcotics Bureau, and the suicide rate is three times the national average. This was even true way back in 1876 when B. E. Lloyd wrote, "Although San Francisco develops more insanity and induces a greater number of suicides, it is withal a pleasant reflection

186

A leading personality of North Beach Bohemia discusses life and literature in one of the cultural centers of that part of the city. (Photo: Jacqueline Paul.)

Although there are some racial problems, of course, there appear to be less than in any other American city. (Photo: Charles Wong.)

Italian crew relaxing on a tuna boat. (Photo: Jacqueline Paul.)

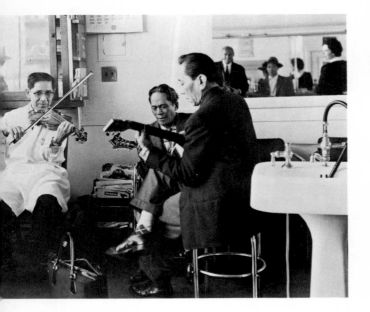

At Dante's Billiard and Lunch Parlor. (Photo: Ione Hyman.)

Left: Only in San Francisco . . . I snapped this group when I heard dulcet tones (well, energetic ones, anyway) emanating from a Kearny Street barber shop. They play every day between shaves.

that she has but few idiots." (A debatable point these days after a short time on the Bayshore freeway.)

Many theories have been offered to account for these curious contradictions. Writer Bruce Bliven, in *Harper's* magazine, came up with as acceptable a theory as any:

> San Franciscans have had a reputation as hard drinkers, going back to the earliest days, and a cultural tradition of this sort is more important than many people realize. The cold, damp climate encourages the consumption of gin and whiskey; even though there is a big Italian colony, and large amounts of excellent wine are made only a few miles away to the north and south, San Franciscans have never become wine drinkers, though they do better than the inhabitants of most other American cities.
>
> California has far more than her normal share of the nation's neurotics and crackpots, the unstable characters who move from community to community. These human tumbleweeds have always had a tendency to drift toward the West, until they pile up along the edge of the Pacific Ocean. Many of them find a spiritual home in the environs of Los Angeles; but some others feel out of place in the brisk go-getter atmosphere of that community, move north four hundred miles, and end up killing themselves, or vegetating among the hopeless drunks of San Francisco's Skid Row. Such, at least, is the theory.

But enough of that; there are some problems in San Francisco, of course. Big ones. But this book was conceived and executed as a flagrant, unabashed valentine, and who amongst us is poltroonish enough to point out his best girl's blemishes on the lacy paper heart he sends her? This book was never intended to be any probing Rorschach of the character of the city and its psyche, no muckraking pamphlet. Certainly, all the views aren't breathtaking in the city, nor all the streets boulevards, nor all the homes beautiful, nor all the people well adjusted and happy. But slum me no slums, and skid me no rows and beat me no niks—not in *this* valentine. Because it's a great city and a beautiful city and if it has problems they're less in evidence than in any other I know.

Portrait of a puzzled constabulary. (Photo: Stoll.)

Here in one photo are six captains of San Francisco finance and industry. Left to right, near camera: J. Sullivan, Jr., of the Crocker-Anglo Bank; James B. Black, of Pacific Gas and Electric Company; Walter A. Haas, of Levi Strauss; J. D. Zellerbach, of the Crown Zeller-bach paper empire; S. Clark Beise, of the Bank of America; Charles R. Blyth of the invest-ment firm of Blyth and Company. (Photo: San Francisco *Chronicle*.)

PERSONALITIES

A glamorous globe-trotting Hollywood personality yawned to me in Beverly Hills not so long ago, "Oh yes, San Francisco's nice, but, really, *who's there?*"

It seems to me there are quite a few people *here,* though maybe they have a different glitter from the ones who are *there.* There are all sorts of defined individuals in this city who are actively engaged in their particular métiers and who contribute to the *ambiance* and feel of our city. Some have already been mentioned and shown in photos—William Saroyan, Kathleen Norris, and Lucius Beebe, for example. In this section of the book and in the next are a few more personalities, though of course it is impossible to include the dozens and dozens of others who ought to be represented.

Left: Mortimer J. Adler, probably our city's most esteemed philosopher. *Below, center:* Roger Lapham, Jr., head of the city's Planning Commission and son of a shipping tycoon and former mayor, with Mrs. Lapham at the Pacific Union Club. This, surely, must be the only published inside photograph of that august edifice—and darn little you can see at that. *Below, right:* Lawyer William R. Wallace, Jr. and his wife, actress Ina Claire, live "down on the Penninsula" but consider themselves San Franciscans. As Herb Caen points out, "You don't have to live in San Francisco to be a San Franciscan." It is more a state of mind than a question of geography.

(Photo: Julian Graham.)

(Photos: San Francisco *Chronicle*.)

Below: Philanthropist and tireless civic leader, Mrs. Nion Tucker (*right*) seems to be on the board of every organization in the city. One of her favorite charities is Guide Dogs for the Blind. *Right:* Christian de Guigne, chairman of the board of Stauffer Chemical Company, and his wife are social leaders in the city and on the Peninsula, where they live. (Photos: San Francisco *Chronicle.*)

Multi-millionaire financier Louis R. Lurie (*left*) and famed trial lawyer J. W. "Jake" Ehrlich. (Photo: George Shimmon.)

Photo: A.P.)

Above: Two generations of Crockers, a historic name in the city. At left, the late William H. Crocker, for forty-three years president of the Crocker First National Bank, and his son, William W. Crocker, who succeeded him. The bank has merged, and is now called the Crocker-Anglo. *Right:* Cyril Magnin, merchant, civic leader, and president of the San Francisco Port Authority.

(Photo: Bill Young.)

(Photo: Bill Young.)

(Photo: George Shimmon.)

(Photo: San Francisco *Chronicle*.)

Top left: Percy King, for years reigning monarch of the debutante Cotillion, is a grandson of newspaper editor James King of William (see page 18). *Above:* Columnist and monologuist Paul Speegle (shown with Mitzi Gaynor) is undisputedly the city's best and funniest M.C. *Left:* Nicol Smith, explorer and lecturer, shown with Mrs. Francis Martin. *Lower left:* Don Sherwood, who bills himself as "the world's greatest disk jockey," and who may well be just that. He is certainly the world's most married one—being a four-time loser at under thirty. Here he is with two of his ex-wives in a jolly get-together. *Below:* Louise Boyd, distinguished Bay Area explorer and Arctic expert, photographed at the airport. (Photo: Pan American.)

Above: Ann Holden, long-time first lady of radio in San Francisco, interviews Marian Anderson. (Photo: Minton.)

Charles Schulz, creator of Schroeder, Lucy, Charlie Brown, and Snoopy, is just about everyone's favorite cartoonist. (Photo: San Francisco *Chronicle*.)

Two of the city's most publicized personalities are ex-madam, now restaurateur, Sally Stanford, and brilliant, controversial labor boss Harry Bridges. (Photo: Campbell.)

George Mardikian, chef par excellence, and owner of the famous Omar Khayyam Restaurant, is shown with his son. (Photo: World Wide.)

SUNDAY

Back in 1876, B. E. Lloyd wrote, "Sunday in San Francisco! Well, what does that signify? A day of rest? Yes; to a few. A holy day? To some. A day of sport, of mirth, of levity, jollity, riot and dissipation? Aye; to many."

People go to church.

(Photo: Paul Hassel.)

194

Some people dig in the garden   (Photo: P. Mozesson.)

. . . or do a little decorating.

(Photo: Ruth Bernhard.)

Others go to the playground at the beach.

Or they go down to the St. Francis Yacht Club to catch some sun—if nothing else

. . . or they brunch at Enrico's coffee house for that European feeling

. . . or else sail over to Sam's
in Tiburon for lunch on deck

(Photo: Ken McLaughlin.)

. . . or play golf as Ken Venturi is doing here at the Harding Park course

. . . or ride down to Pebble Beach to watch the finals

(Photo: Bill You

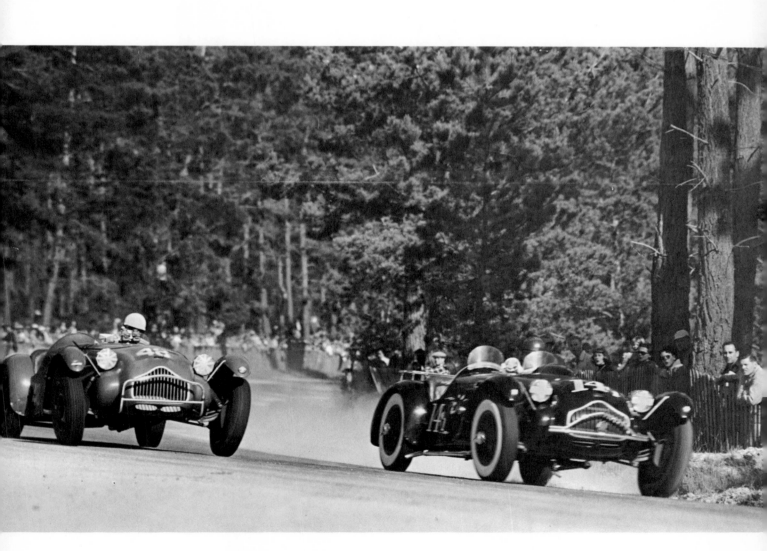

. . . or buzz over to Monterey for the sports-car races   (Photo: Julian P. Graham.)

. . . and, after golf or the races, go over to friends for lunch or tea and socializing, as the Windsors are doing here at the George Coleman house

. . . or go to the Burlingame Country Club on the former Crocker estate

(Photo: Jerome Zerbe.)

. . . or perhaps be the guests of Mr. and Mrs. Charles Blyth at "Strawberry Hill." Shown with them here are Raymond Armsby and Edmunds Lyman.

Ball-game fans watch Willie Mays clout one for the Giants at Candlestick Point ball park. Before the Giants arrived, the old team was called the Seals, and way back the ball club was known as (horrors) the "Friscoes"!

(Photo: Ken McLaughlin.)

Equestrians watch polo in the park—played here by George Pope (of Pope and Talbot steamship line) and Charlie Low (owner of the Forbidden City)

(Photo:
San Francisco *Chronicle*.)

. . . and they go wild at the Cow Palace rodeo. The Cow Palace is the largest indoor arena in the West. It is valued at $50,000,000, and can accommodate more than 17,000 people but only 8000 cows.

Skiers meet at the Sugar Bowl or, as here, at Squaw Valley, site of the 1960 Olympic Games.

(Photo: Dick Skuse.)

And sooner or later everyone takes photos of the Cid outside the Palace of
the Legion of Honor after enjoying the paintings on display in the museum

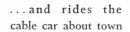

...and rides the
cable car about town

(Photo: Ruth Bernhard.)

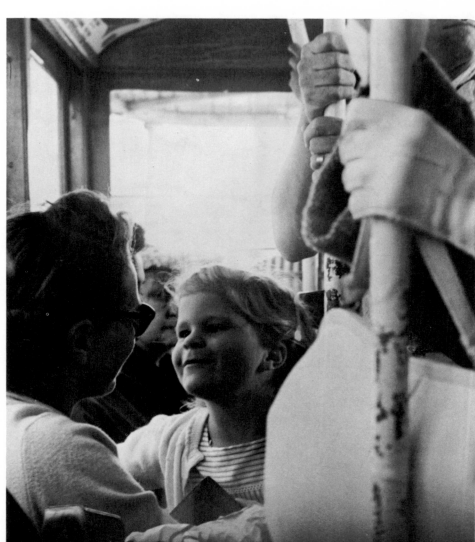

. . . or goes to the zoo. The Fleishhacker Zoo, one of the finest in the country, features moatlike enclosures which give the illusion of no confinement at all.

On a Sunday you can drive to Sequoia National Park,
or take a run in the Presidio woods like this little girl

. . . or simply stay home and let yourself go in the backyard.

(Photos: Miriam Young.)

LOVERS

(Photos: Jacqueline Paul.)

(Photo: San Francisco *Examiner*.)

EPILOGUE

So here is the end of our portrait of "the cool grey city of love," as George Sterling called it.

If it had been a better book—as Mr. Hemingway did it in that sneaky, contrived, great last chapter in *Death in the Afternoon*—it would have more, so much more.

If it had turned out the way one could idealize it, the book would have delved deeper into the fascinating early history of the city. It would have told more of the Spanish way of life, more of the Mission Dolores, more of the pioneers. It would have told about the duels, and the justice meted out to the crook with the wonderful name Philander Brace by the Second Vigilantes, and it would have had rollicking bawdy stories of the Barbary Coast, apocryphal or not. It certainly should have investigated the goings-on in an actual *maison de chat* of the time appallingly named and advertised as "Ye Olde Whore Shoppe."

And the political machinations through the years—it would be loaded with anecdotes about them. And it would have discussed all the mayors at length from Geary to Rolph to Christopher.

And Tom Mooney—one should have at least mentioned the Mooney case. And all the delectable murders that have taken place in the city—like that chap Durrant who did away with the beautiful girl in the church belfry.

And the "China Boys" who were "part of the family"—they should have rated some space.

212

And Mammy Pleasant is barely mentioned, and how about Tait's and Robert's at the Beach, and Adolph Sutro, and what about the semi-imaginary bandit Joaquin Murrieta?

And the many really good young writers and artists who didn't even get mentioned, how about that? And not much on the Peninsula, or the interiors of fancy houses in the city, and no pictures of the University of California or Stanford or Galileo and Lowell High.

Or the developments on the fringe of the city like Park Merced and Stonestown—shouldn't they have rated a picture?

If the book had really been everything that San Francisco is to me, it would have had a photo of F.D.R.'s motorcade going down Van Ness, and Willie Mays' coming up Montgomery Street. And a nice smoky photo of the old Tahitian Hut on lower Broadway with Terangi doing his knife dance and the Goupil brothers barking out, "Vana Vana." And Mona's downstairs rat's nest and the vanished La Fiesta, where the big act was the man who stayed on stage for an hour pouring down customers' drinks, and then wobbled to the men's room, became sick, and emerged all ready for the next show. And Ted Lewis at Bimbo's, and Griff Williams, Anson Weeks, Art Hickman, and Tom Coakley at the hotels. And there should have been a sort of woozy photo of the interior of Sally Stanford's *palais de joie* with Sally and the girls.

And a photo of a bunch of happy kids' faces, mine among them, watching Tony Sarg's marionettes at the old Paul Elder's shop, or at a matinee of *Mister Antonio* starring Leo Carrillo, or a birthday-party clown in the theater room of the de Young mansion on California Street, which had a real stage for home entertainment.

And what about Octagon House on Gough Street? And there should have been more than a mention of the City of Paris, San Francisco's oldest department store, and of the Emporium, the largest store in northern California, and of all the fine book shops besides Paul Elder's that cater to San Franciscan literary taste. And what about the New York stores that have also become San Franciscan—Macy's, Brooks Brothers, and Saks Fifth Avenue?

Yes, it should have had all this and more.

But, even then, would it have been any more than San Francisco to one man? Maybe it's not possible for a book to capture what the city means to all men. I shall console myself with that thought. And with Caen's "San Francisco, yours and mine, nobody's and everybody's—always moving away just as you reach out to touch it."

Kipling said, "San Francisco has only one drawback—'tis hard to leave."

And leave we must, for it is the end of the book and time to leave the city where, Frank Norris claimed, "almost anything can happen."

Thirty-seven years ago, I was so taken by the physical and spiritual climate of San Francisco that I decided to be born here, and I hope I have the foresight and good taste to die here. My children used their heads and also got themselves born in San Francisco, and I hope that their children, despite the blatant blandishments of Paris, Madrid, or Tahiti, will do likewise; for here is a regal, ever-exciting, proud, old-young place which never ceases to thrill.

STREET NAMES

By DALE CONRAD

Street naming seems to be one of the most haphazard processes in San Francisco history. According to Robert O'Brien, most streets are named by "one or two persons, the engineer who lays them out or the person who owns the land bordering the new thoroughfare." To this list should be added contractors for subdivisions, friends and relatives of surveyors, and, in the old days, town councilmen, their friends and relatives, and a very interesting unknown quantity of people who answered an ad inserted in 1849 by the city surveyor, William Eddy, which stated that if anyone wanted a street named after him all he had to do was deposit a case of champagne at Mr. Eddy's office with his calling card enclosed.

Mr. O'Brien says that the next step in the street-naming process is this: "The selected names are then referred to the Department of Public Works, Building Permit Bureau, division in charge of house numbering, an obscure branch of the municipal government, which sees to it that people number their houses right . . . and not after their favorite lottery ticket"

When Jasper O'Farrell named the streets in 1847, the town was smaller (population around 450) and there were no Public Works. Most names were suggested and chewed over by the alcalde and his councilmen.

Matthew Turner says in his *Builders of a Great City* (1891) that Alcaldes Bartlett and Hyde "had a good deal to do with the street nomenclature"; they were responsible for Stockton, Montgomery, Mason, Fremont, Kearny, Geary, Sutter, O'Farrell, and Dupont Streets. An interesting sidelight: "California was first called Market Street but in February, 1847, Alcalde Bryant changed it to California St." And "Broadway was so-called because it was thought that it would be similar in importance to its great namesake in New York."

The first map and survey of San Francisco, then Yerba Buena, was made by Jean Jacques Vioget in 1839. He laid out five very narrow streets—only 49 feet wide, running east to west: Jackson, Washington, Pacific, Clay, and Sacramento. Vioget seemed to be lacking in the sense of *grands boulevards* of the Paris street planners. His survey extended west to Stockton Street, north to Vallejo Street, and south to California Street.

In 1847 Jasper O'Farrell improved the survey and street engineering and even shifted Market Street at a 2½-degree angle (called "O'Farrell's swing"). In 1849, William Eddy made another map. After that, streets were added as needed and named after the surveyor's best friend at the time.

There developed great confusion and irregularity in postal deliveries due to duplication of names (there was a Virginia Street, a Virginia Avenue, a Virginia Place, and a Virginia Court). Important thoroughfares were being called streets and unimportant streets were being called avenues; and there were hardly any decent street signs. Finally, in 1909, a group of citizens gathered together to recommend street-name changes and more proper signs so that "strangers may readily find their way." In this group were Zoeth Eldredge, historian, and other alert citizens such as Charles Murdock, W. W Sanderson, J. D. McGilvray, R. W. Madden, Charles Sedgwick Aitken, and Henry Payot.

They managed to do a lot of name cleaning as well as to add some new ones—a long list from "Anza to Yorba," running in alphabetical order parallel to Ocean Beach in the Sunset District. Confusion from duplications was diminished (now there is only Virginia Avenue left out of the terrible four), but confusion still existed and led to peculiar situations. There was a Yerba Buena Avenue and a Yerba Buena Street, so, to simplify matters, the story goes, an official decided to change the name of the smaller thoroughfare, actually an alley, on Nob Hill. For a long time Mrs. William Sproule, owner of the property on the alley and descendant of a pioneer family, objected strenuously and vociferously to changing the historic name. But then a Solomon of an official suggested a completely acceptable alternative, and the signpost soon read "Sproule Lane."

The following is a list of typical street names in San Francisco, and of the names most asked about, plus information about them and why some deserved to be preserved on street signs. The streets obviously named for trees, presidents, and Greek mythological characters are not listed, nor are many names whose origins are obscure. Most streets in San Francisco are named after the aforementioned and pioneers (anyone who came to California before 1850), military and naval heroes, town officials, ships that arrived in the pioneer period, Indian tribes, Spanish settlers and Spanish words, some women of questionable reputation or identity, and surveyors and their friends. Jean Jacques Vioget seems to be the only surveyor who did not get his name on a street sign.

A researcher can find out if a street is named after a certain person only if a statement was made to that effect either in town-meeting records or by a member of a family who remembers that his great-aunt somebody was named on a street sign.

Authorities heavily referred to in making up this list are Henry Carlisle (*San Francisco Street Names*); Albert Wheelan ("The Streets, Avenues, Alleys, and Lanes of South of Market," published in the *South of Market Journal*, April 1929); Zoeth Eldredge (*Beginnings of San Francisco*); *The City Directories*; H. H. Bancroft (*History of California*); and Mr. James deT. Abajian, the Librarian for the California Historical Society in San Francisco, who is a pre-cybernetic marvel of a walking, talking card-index system.

Albion Street. Sir Frances Drake labeled California on his maps in 1579 "Nova Albion."

Alemany Boulevard. Joseph Alemany: first Roman Catholic archbishop of San Francisco, 1853-1884.

Anna Lane. According to folklore, the two Lane brothers divided their lot by a coin flip, the winner receiving the choice of either half, and the loser the remainder and the dubious privilege of naming the street the lot was on. The loser's daughter was Anna Lane.

Alvarado Street. Juan Bautista Alvarado: Mexican governor of California, 1836-1842.

Anza Boulevard. Don Juan Bautista de Anza: leader of settlers to Monterey and establisher of Presidio of San Francisco, 1776.

Arguello Boulevard. The Argüello family played a prominent role in California history during the Mexican regime and after. José was commanding officer at the Presidio (1787-1806). His brother, Don Santiago, held public office in Los Angeles. José's son was Luis Antonio, first governor of Alta California and owner of land extending from San Francisco to Palo Alto. Santaguito aided Commodore Robert E. Stockton in the conquest of California. (The other noted pro-American Mexican was General Vallejo.) María Concepción had a sad love affair with a Russian count, Nicolai Rezanov (see the historical novel by Gertrude Atherton, *Rezanov*).

Balance Street. According to Walter Brooks, whose grandfather, Benjamin S. Brooks, arrived on the ship *Balance*, the street was named after the ship, which lies buried there.

Bartlett Street. Washington A. Bartlett: first alcalde of San Francisco, 1846.

Battery Street. Captain Montgomery placed a battery of guns here in 1846.

Beale Street. Edward F. Beale was a brave lieutenant under General Kearny during the American conquest of California. But he is more humorously famous for his attempt to establish a wagon road from Fort Defiance, Arizona, into Southern California, using camels. The project failed because of the beasts' nasty dispositions, and when they arrived in the Bay area they were sold to be used in the Nevada silver mines.

Bernal Avenue. Juan Francisco Bernal: soldier who came with de Anza in 1776 and later became owner of a ranch of 4400 acres, including parts of San Francisco and San Mateo County.

Brannan Street. Samuel Brannan, a famous firster, performed the first marriage (Mormon) under the American flag in San Francisco (1847), campaigned for and made the first donation to the first public school in San Francisco, was the first to announce to the world the discovery of gold at Sutter's Mill (1848), became San Francisco's first millionaire, and organized the first Vigilante Committee (1851).

Breen Place. Patrick Breen: One of the few survivors of the ill-fated Donner party, who wrote the record of the ordeal, *Diary of the Donner Party*.

Bret Harte Terrace. Harte became famous as editor of the *Overland Monthly*, which first published his "The Heathen Chinee" and "San Francisco from the Sea."

Broderick Street. David C. Broderick: United States senator in the 1850s who died in a pistol duel with David S. Terry, chief justice of State Supreme Court. Ten thousand mourned Broderick at his funeral, and it has been said that this was the "last great pistol duel in San Francisco."

Bryant Street. Edwin C. Bryant: alcalde of San Francisco, 1847.

Buchanan Street. Henry Carlisle claims that this street was named *not* after President James Buchanan, but after John C. Buchanan, a prominent citizen of the 1850s, because the street was so named and listed in the San Francisco Directory in 1856, before Buchanan was elected President.

Bush Street. Carlisle thinks this street might have been named after an assistant (J. P. Bush) to Jasper O'Farrell who mapped and named streets in 1847. But Matthew Turner writes in 1891 that Mr. Hyde (an alcalde) gave Bush Street its name on account of the number of bushes growing there. Cartographers sometimes mispell the name as Busch, but we find no such person in the early directories. This street is probably the biggest mystery to street-name investigators.

Cabrillo Street. Juan Rodríguez Cabrillo: a navigator. The street was named by the 1909 committee of citizens for changing street names.

Carolina Street. See Harriet Street.

Clay Street. After Henry or road conditions.

Davidson Street. George Davidson: government surveyor, physicist, and professor at the University of California before the 1900s.

Davis Street. William Heath Davis: author of *75 Years in California,* recognized as one of the most detailed descriptions of early California history.

de Boom Street. Cornelius de Boom: pioneer (came to San Francisco before 1850) and real-estate agent.

Divisadero Street. From the Spanish word meaning a "look-out point."

Drumm Street. Lieutenant Richard Coulton Drumm: United States Army officer, important enough in the 1850s.

DuBoce Street. An important thoroughfare, but there is no record of whom it is named after. Possibly a Major Victor DuBoce who was described in the *Western Soldier* magazine (1891) as a "popular . . . member of several social and secret orders . . . also Post Office Superintendent." These credentials may be enough to warrant a street's being named after one?

Dupont Street. Admiral Samuel F. DuPont: Naval hero. Now Grant Avenue (after Ulysses), it was originally Calle de la Fundación until 1846, when it was called "Dupont" (though the Admiral spelled it Du Pont). When the ruins were cleared away after the quake, the street namers decided a clean slate was due notoriously wicked Dupont Street. The Admiral was highly important in California naval history; the name should be used again for a more important thoroughfare (avenue or boulevard).

Eddy Street. William M. Eddy: city surveyor, 1849, who made the next map after O'Farrell's.

Ellis Street. Alfred J. Ellis: prominent pioneer and town councilman in the 1850s.

Embarcadero. From the Spanish word meaning "embarking place"

Fairfax Avenue. "Lord" Charles Snowden Fairfax: owner of land now called Fairfax, Marin County.

Fallon Place. Thomas Fallon: one of the leaders of the Bear Flag Revolt (1846).

217

Franklin Street. Is this named for Benjamin, or for Selim, an early realtor (as suggested by Carlisle)?

Fremont Street. Colonel John C. Frémont: a United States conqueror of California; later a United States senator (1850), and candidate for the presidency (1856).

Fulton Street. Possibly named for a pioneer, Daniel J. (1849), as well as the inventor, Robert.

Garden Street. Named after the Russ Gardens, according to a letter to Robert O'Brien's *Chronicle* column ("Rip Tides") from Bill Gutzkow, grandson of Charles Russ, owner of the "gardens."

Geary Street. John W. Geary: first mayor under 1850 City Charter and donor of land to city, now called Union Square.

Golden Gate Avenue. So named because it leads to Golden Gate Park. (This name really makes sense!)

Gough Street. Charles H. Gough: prominent citizen in 1850s who served on a committee for naming streets.

Grant Avenue. See Dupont Street.

Green Street. Talbot H. Green: prominent citizen who held many offices, and while running for mayor (in the 1850s) was accused of actually being a Paul Geddes, embezzler, whereupon he left town for good. (The street name stayed.)

Guerrero Street. Francisco Guerrero: early Spanish settler and landowner.

Haight Street. Named after one of the members of the Haight family, which included bankers, lawyers, and pioneers.

Halleck Street. General Henry W. Halleck: Army officer who built the famous Montgomery Block building in 1853, torn down in May 1959.

Harriet Street. Jasper O'Farrell designated the lots south of Market Street to be four times the size of the blocks north of Market, so they were divided by small streets for better access. Most of the streets are named for women—who some say were relatives or sweethearts of early pioneers pining away for home; others say they were favorite madams or mistresses. Mr. Bill Gutzkow, however, wrote uprighteously to Robert O'Brien, of the *Chronicle*, that "This st. [Harriet] was named after my Aunt Harriet Russ and the other street—Carolina—after Carolina Russ. Both these ladies most highly respected, passed away in early life."

Harrison Street. Named either after the President or after a merchant and town councilman, Edward H.

Hayes Street. Named after a prominent family including active citizens such as Colonel Thomas and Michael.

Howard Street. William Howard: wealthy merchant and civic leader in the 1850s.

Hyde Street. George Hyde: alcalde of Yerba Buena after Bartlett (1846).

Jones Street. Named after Commodore Thomas A. Jones, who first planted the American flag in California soil in 1842, capturing Monterey, says Matthew Turner. Named after a lawyer, Elbert P., says Carlisle. Named after Doctor Elbert P., who was first editor of the *California Star* and member of the 1847 Town Council, says Eldredge. (Who knows? There are plenty of Joneses.)

Judah Street. Theodore Judah: pioneer, 1826-1863.

Kearny Street. General Stephen Watts Kearny: a United States conqueror of California, later military governor of California (1847). The street is *not* named after Dennis Kearney, a rabble-rouser in the 1870s.

Larkin Street. Thomas Oliver Larkin: United States consul in Monterey in the 1840s and later a large landowner in San Francisco.

Laguna Street. Near the extinct "Washerwomen's Lagoon," where gold-rushers did their laundry.

Leavenworth Street. Thaddeus M. Leavenworth: chaplain and consul in San Francisco (1848-1849).

Leese Street. Jacob Primer Leese: built one of the first houses in Yerba Buena (1836).

Leidesdorff Street. William A. Leidesdorff: United States vice-consul at Yerba Buena when taken by Montgomery. He built the first hotel, on the corner of California and Leidesdorff Streets.

Lick Place. James Lick: bought sandlots, including land now Montgomery Street, before the Gold Rush. Died leaving $3,500,000. Donated a major share to the building of the Lick Observatory and the Lick-Wilmerding Polytechnic School.

Lyon Street. Captain Nathaniel Lyon: avenged the murder by Indians of Captain William H. Warner.

Macondray Lane. Frederick Macondray: merchant. Emperor Norton reputedly bought a large cargo of rice from him and, after the rice market collapsed, the demented Norton tried to marry Macondray's daughter to make her an empress in lieu of paying the shipping bill.

Maiden Lane. First it was called St. Mark's Lane, a contrast to the infamous Iodoform Kate who ruled over the blocks of the thoroughfare. Then Morton Street (1865), after the Morton Hotel. In 1909 it was changed to Union Square Avenue; in 1921 to Manila Street; then, in 1922, to Maiden Lane, at the request of Albert Samuels, jewelry-store owner who wanted the street named after the famous jewelry street in London.

Main Street. Not our biggest and most important street, it is named after Charles Main, a pioneer in 1849, according to Wheelan.

Market Street. Named after the same street in Philadelphia and laid out by O'Farrell, originally a Philadelphian.

Mason Street. Colonel Richard B. Mason: military governor of California, 1847-1849.

McAllister Street. Hall McAllister: famous lawyer in the 1850s.

Mesa Street. Juan Prado Mesa: Mexican commander who quelled an Indian rebellion (1831) in Santa Clara, led by Yoscolo, a notoriously scheming fellow, who was killed and beheaded. Yoscolo's head was placed on a pole in front of the mission as a warning to other obstreperous Indians.

Mission Street traces the original route between Yerba Buena and the Mission Dolores.

Montgomery Street. Captain John B. Montgomery: commander of the *Portsmouth,* who raised the United States flag in Yerba Buena Plaza on July 9, 1846.

Natoma Street. Originally named after Henry Mellus, who sold out to his partner in

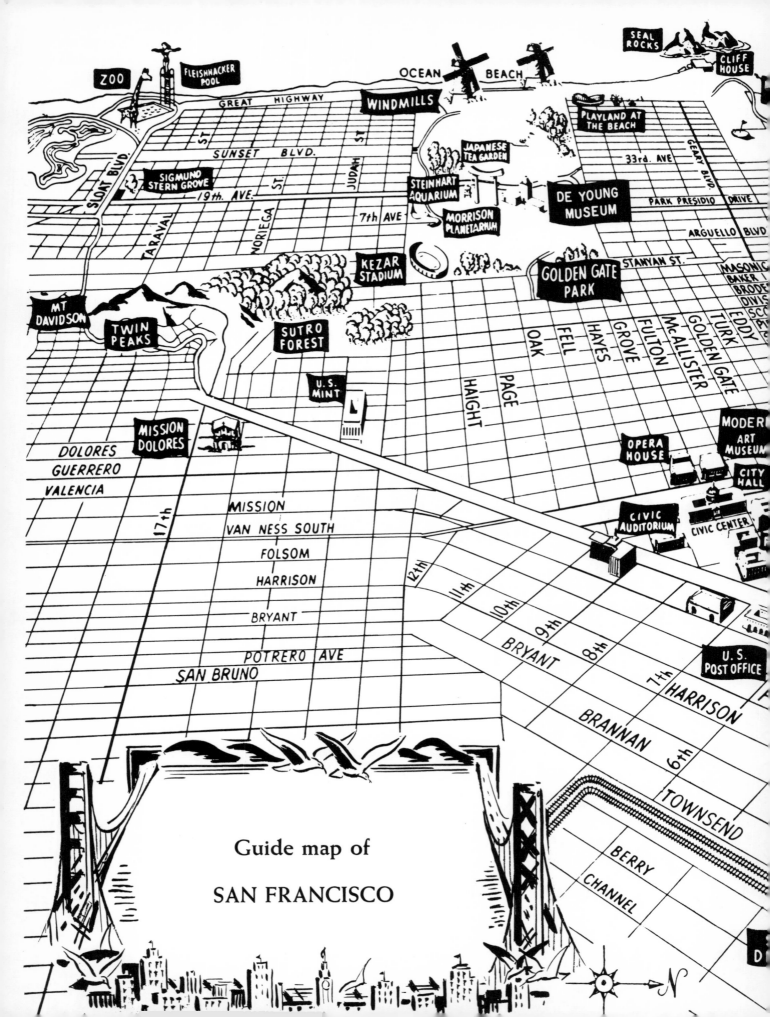

Guide map of

SAN FRANCISCO

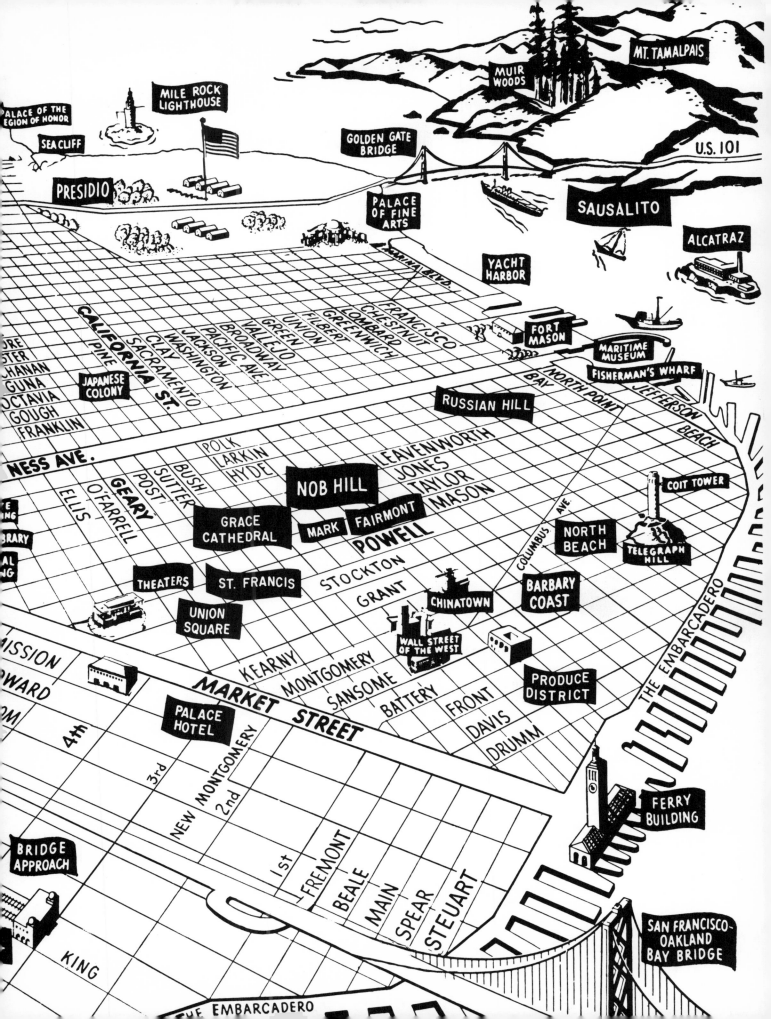

business, William Howard, after an attack of apoplexy. He later stated that he was not paid the fair value of his property. Howard, angered by Mellus's accusations, caused the street name to be changed to Natoma—the name of an Indian tribe on the American River.

New Montgomery Street was cut through to Market from Montgomery Street (1868-1869). The land for the street was donated to the city by A. P. Harpending and W. T. Sharon.

Noe Street. José Noe: Spanish owner of the San Miguel Ranch (4000 acres) in the center of San Francisco.

Noriega Street. José de la Guerra y Noriega: Spanish land grantee, owner of lands in Contra Costa and Marin several square miles in size.

North Point Street. Named after the old North Point that existed before the fill (near the intersection of Kearny and North Point Streets).

Octavia Street. Miss Octavia Gough: sister of Charles Gough, who was on the commission for laying out and naming streets in the 1850s.

O'Farrell Street. Jasper O'Farrell made the first map of San Francisco (1847) after Jean Jacques Vioget (1839).

Ophir Alley. Named after the gold mine?

Ortega Street. José Francisco de Ortega: scout of Portolá who first saw the Golden Gate.

Page Street. The Pages are an old San Francisco family but Eldredge says the street was named after Robert C. Page, a town clerk (1851-1856).

Palou Street. Fra Francisco Palou: first padre of San Francisco Mission, noted for his biography of Junípero Serra, famous Spanish missionary in California.

Parrott Alley. Probably named after the old San Francisco family of merchants and bankers.

Peralta Avenue. The Peraltas were Spanish settlers who came to California with Anza and owned a ranch of 49,000 acres, now the cities of Oakland, Alameda, and Berkeley.

Pico Avenue. Pio Pico: last Mexican Governor of California (1845-1846).

Portolá Drive. Gaspar de Portolá: first Spanish governor of California, who founded the Presidio of Monterey and discovered San Francisco Bay, 1769.

Portsmouth Square. Named after the United States man-of-war *Portsmouth*, captained by Montgomery.

Post Street. Gabriel B. Post: merchant, city official, and state senator in the 1840s and 1850s.

Potrero Avenue. Named after the Spanish word meaning "stock grazing land."

Quesada Avenue. Gonzálo Ximénez de Quesada: Spanish explorer; name chosen by 1909 street-naming commission.

Quintara Street. Eldredge says Quintara was the name of an old Spanish family. But Charles Murdock says there is no such family. He has only heard of a mulatto, Luis Quintero, "who was sent away from the pueblo [Los Angeles] for general worthlessness." Both Eldredge and Murdock served on the 1909 street-naming commission.

Richardson Street. William A. Richardson: an Englishman, the first dweller in Yerba

Buena (1835), and the original owner of the land that is now Sausalito.

Rincon Place. Rincón means "corner" in Spanish. The southern point of Yerba Buena Cove was originally called Rincon Point.

Russ Street. J. C. Christian Russ: an early jeweler and owner of a hotel very close to the present Russ Building.

Sanchez Street. Sánchez was the name of a family owning large ranchos, 24,000 acres, extending from South San Francisco to Burlingame.

Santiago Street. Santiago: a Spanish battle cry, according to Eldredge, chosen as street name by the 1909 commission.

Scott Street. Probably named after General Winfield Scott. No authority is certain.

Serra Boulevard. Fra Junípero Serra established the first mission in Alta California at San Diego in 1769, and subsequently was head of all missions in California.

Sloat Boulevard. Commodore John D. Sloat: commander of the United States Pacific Naval Squadron who recaptured Monterey from the Mexicans in 1846.

Sparrow Alley. According to Wheelan named by neighborhood boys for their "nemesis 'Old Man Sparrow.' "

Spear Street. Carlisle says it was named after Nathan Spear, a pioneer (1832) and merchant.

Stanyan Street. Charles A. Stanyan: one of the members of an "Outside Lands Committee" who were responsible for choosing the site of the Golden Gate Park.

Steiner Street. The published obituary of L. Steiner (1911) states that this street was named for him.

Steuart Street. William M. Steuart: a town official in the 1850s.

Stevenson Street. Colonel Jonathan Drake Stevenson: commander of the New York Volunteers (1847).

Stockton Street. Commodore Robert F. Stockton: successor to Commodore Sloat and later military governor of California (1846).

Sutter Street. John A. Sutter: owner of land near Coloma where John Marshall found gold (1848).

Taraval Street. Taraval: an Indian guide in Anza's expedition.

Tehama Street. Another letter from Bill Gutzkow: "In the 90's this st. was made quite famous for the reason that many chorus girls of the old Tivoli Opera House on Eddy St. lived on it. To compete with the wealthy females on Nob Hill who were bedecked with diamonds and sealskins—these girls wore an imitation sealskin fabricated from cat fur and dog skins. It was called 'Tehama sealskin'." Tehama is also the name of an Indian tribe.

Thomas Street. Named by the 1909 commission. General George Henry Thomas was known as "the Rock of Chickamauga." Why didn't they choose the latter name?

Tovar Avenue. Don Pedro Tovar: ensign-general in Coronado's army. Choice of the 1909 commission.

Townsend Street. Dr. John Townsend: president of the Town Council, 1847.

Turk Street. Frank Turk: lawyer and city official of the pioneer period.

Ugarte Street. Fra John Ugarte: founder of missions in Lower California (late seventeenth century).

Ulloa Street. Francisco de Ulloa: a Spanish navigator.

Valencia Street. Candelario Valencia: one of Anza's soldiers and large ranch owner in Contra Costa County.

Vallejo Street. General Mariano Guadalupe Vallejo: Mexican comandante in Presidio, San Francisco, and later Sonoma. Called "the best friend the United States had in California."

Van Dyke Avenue. Walter Van Dyke: a justice of the Supreme Court in California. Choice of the 1909 commission.

Van Ness Avenue. James Van Ness: mayor of San Francisco, 1846.

Wawona Street. Wawona: an Indian name, but who was she?

Webster Street. Named after Noah, or the statesman?

Yorba Street. Antonio Yorba: soldier with the Anza expedition.

Zoe Street. Zoe: a girl, but who was she? Another of the thousands of mysteries which abound in the history of a fascinating city.

The burned area of San Francisco in 1906 (*top right*) plotted on a map of the entire city. (Courtesy Wells Fargo Bank.)

INDEX

(See also alphabetical list of street names beginning on page 214.)

225

227